# Cars of the Fantastic '50s

©2005 Dan Lyons
Published by

**kp books**
*An Imprint of F+W Publications*

**700 East State Street • Iola, WI 54990-0001**
**715-445-2214 • 888-457-2873**

Our toll-free number to place an order or obtain
a free catalog is (800) 258-0929.

Library of Congress Catalog Number: 2005906837

ISBN: 0-87349-926-3

Designed by Gary Carle
Edited by Tom Collins

Printed in China

## Dedication

For Catherine, James and Nancy, with thanks and much love.

## Acknowledgments

I'm grateful to all the owners who allowed me to photograph the beautiful cars and trucks found in this book:

Carl and Mary Allen, Roy Asbahr, Bill and Sandy Atchinson, Charlene and Gil Beckner, Bill Bouchers, Bill Braga, George L. Brownell II, Albert and Gloria Ciejka, Lew Dandurand, John Delap, Jack Garofal, Hector Giancarlo, Jack Gillette, Jeff Goodwin, Frank Hardick, Bob Heuer, Jack and Mary Kelly, John Kepich, John and Darcy Knapp, Rocky Mancini, Ed McCormick, Bob McIntyre, Bill Miller, Ed Miller, Ralph and Gayle Nocera, the Patch Collection, Ronn Pittman, Paul and Yvonne Rhoads, Al Romano Jr., Jess and Rita Ruffalo, the Sarasota Museum of Cars and Music, Bob Schmidt, Tom Scuccimara, Bob Sekelsky, Gerald Sichel, Donald E. Smith, Ed and Kaylene Souers, Al Staley, John Stoodley, Larry Swiggart, Glenn Tyler, Vincent Ucci Jr., John Walker, Lloyd Watts, Edith and Parker Wickham, Butch Wiegold, James and Ruth Wilson and Richard S. Zimmerman.

# Cars of the Fantastic '50s / Contents

# 1950
# Buick Roadmaster

LOOKING AT this Buick's grille, what do you see? The face of Buick's finest for 1950 was controversial – a rolling ink blot test, for prospective car buyers.

Beneath the gun sight hood ornament lay a grille that seemed to spill over the bumper. Buick likened the look to cascading water. Some thought that the effect was less a call to nature than it was a cry for orthodontics. In conservative times, controversy doesn't sell, so Buick's designers made quick work of the metallic malocclusion. The grille receded behind the bumper again the following year. But ironically, the rare, one-year look has since been embraced by many Buick lovers.

Top shelf for Buick for much of the Fifties was Roadmaster. And so, the top "drop top" was the $2,981 Roadmaster convertible. As the flagship of the 1950 line, Roadmaster was decked out with all of Buick's trademark styling cues. Atop the front fenders were "ventiports" – Buick-speak for what the rest of us knew as portholes. This trim first appeared on Buicks in 1949 and like military insignia, the more you had, the higher your rank. Specials and Supers rated three ventiports, and only Roadmaster carried four. Below the ports, a great, chrome sweep spear stretched from the rear haunches to a point just over the front wheels. In back, tailfins had sprouted on Cadillacs in 1948, but the first hint of fin

▲ *Buick's 1950 Roadmaster convertible looked just as good from behind.*

◄ *Buick went to great lengths to justify the Roadmaster's toothy grille. Ads proclaimed the bumper design made parking and garaging easier—though not easier on the garage!*

Liberal use of chrome ▶
lent a jukebox look to the
Roadmaster's radio.

**THIS IS ROADMASTER AT ITS GAYEST**—
*the 126¼-inch-wheelbase Convertible, with push-button
hydraulic control of the weathertight top, the windows
and the front-seat adjustment.*

# For Life, Liberty
## and the Pursuit of Happiness

PERHAPS only in this land of ours can such words mean something else beside man's inalienable rights.

Something, say, like this sweeping beauty of an automobile, where such words also truly belong.

It has life, rich and eager—welling up with instant response from a big 152-hp straight-eight Fireball engine.

It offers freedom—from clutch-pedal pushing, from gearshifting, from the tiring strain of traffic crawls—because every Buick ROADMASTER is bounty-blessed with Dynaflow Drive.

Even freedom from the usual jars and jolts of road roughness is yours in this traveler—for here is the Buick ride of all-coil springing, pillowy tires on broad rims, a keel-steadying torque-tube.

So your way here is clear in the pursuit of fun and happiness and the exciting life.

And you go cloaked in the sweetest style lines of the times. You command ROADMASTER power, size, room and comfort — know a new feeling of freedom and breath-taking joy.

All this can be sampled, at your Buick dealer's, without obligation. Why not discover how much unhampered happiness can be yours in any ROADMASTER model by dropping in to see him soon? Like today—or tomorrow at the latest.

BUICK *Division of* GENERAL MOTORS

**Only BUICK has** *Dynaflow* **and with it goes:**

HIGHER-COMPRESSION Fireball valve-in-head power in three engines. (New F-263 engine in SUPER models.) NEW-PATTERN STYLING, with MULTI-GUARD forefront, taper-through fenders, "double bubble" taillights WIDE-ANGLE VISIBILITY, close-up road view both forward and back • TRAFFIC-HANDY SIZE, less over-all length for easier parking and garaging, short turning radius • EXTRA-WIDE SEATS cradled between the axles SOFT BUICK RIDE, from all-coil springing, Safety-Ride rims, low-pressure tires, ride-steadying torque-tube WIDE ARRAY OF MODELS with Body by Fisher.
*Dynaflow Drive is standard on ROADMASTER, optional at extra cost on SUPER and SPECIAL models.*

*Your Key to Greater Value*

**FOUR-WAY FOREFRONT**
*This rugged front end (1) sets the style note, (2) saves on repair costs — vertical bars are individually replaceable, (3) avoids "locking horns," (4) makes parking and garaging easier.*

*When better automobiles are built BUICK will build them*

# Buick Roadmaster
### with Dynaflow Drive

*First of the Fine Cars in Value*

*Tune in HENRY J. TAYLOR, ABC Network, every Monday evening.*

wouldn't be found on a Buick until 1952. Under the hood, Roadmaster was powered by a 320-cubic-inch, 134-hp straight-eight engine (V-8s were still three years away). Standard in Roadmaster and optional elsewhere in the lineup was Buick's Dynaflow automatic transmission. Its pension for leisurely shifts ultimately earned the gearbox the nickname, "Dynaslush."

Inside, passengers were swaddled in genuine leather, and looked out on a chrome-laden dashboard, with aircraft inspired styling. "Buick's the fashion for 1950" shouted the sales brochures, and the company did indeed seem to be in vogue, with total sales that ranked fourth industry-wide for the year. In a lineup that spanned 19 models, none went down the highway any nicer than a Roadmaster ragtop. Weighing 4,345 lbs. and stretching nearly 215 inches long, just 2,964 were built for 1950.

▲ *Top shelf for Buick for much of the Fifties was Roadmaster.*

◄ *Even the best Buick wouldn't trade its Fireball straight-eight for a V-8 until 1953.*

**1950 Buick Roadmaster** | 9

# Ford Crestliner

CRESTLINER WAS ALL ABOUT the grand art of misdirection.

Late in 1949, General Motors brought out the first "hardtop convertibles." These were steel-topped, two-door coupes, built without B-pillars – the thin, metal bars that traditionally separated front and rear side windows. The idea was to get the airy feel of a convertible (sun and fun!), without the ragtop's drawbacks (leaks and drafts!). GM introduced the new style in their midyear models from Buick, Oldsmobile and Cadillac, then rolled hardtops into the mainstream Chevy lineup the following year.

Suddenly, Ford had a problem—they had no hardtop. And, in the middle of a three-year styling cycle (the popular "shoebox" cars of 1949 through 1951), they had no prospects of having one any time soon. Caught in the unenviable position of not matching, model for model, with its cross-town competition, Ford found a solution in some sleight of hand. They created a quick fix, called Crestliner. The Crestliner was a Tudor sedan notable for its eye-popping, two-tone colors, and bold, contrast sweep gracing the slab sides. The complementary hue was also restated on the vinyl top, which was padded, to emulate a convertible. Exterior

◄ *The hood ornament seemed to point the way for 1950 Ford Crestliner drivers.*

*The Crestliner's Deluxe interior was color-keyed to its bright exterior hues. Seats were done in broadcloth and vinyl with a four-spoke wheel standard in this series only.*

highlights also included fender skirts, dressy hubcaps and the Crestliner script, wrought in anodized gold. Inside, the dual color combinations were repeated in upgraded fabrics.

Bright colors and extroverted two-toning would become styling staples of the Fifties, but mainly *later* in the Fifties, post 1955. In 1950, Crestliner was riding ahead of the curve. Packing Ford's venerable flathead V-8 under the hood and selling for $1,711, the colorful coupes held the line by holding customer interest until the real, "no post" deal arrived in 1951. (It was rushed ahead of Ford's scheduled 1952 debut by GM's hardtop "first strike" in 1949.) Crestliner returned for 1951 with much less fanfare. After all, now that true hardtops were a part of the lineup, the Crestliner's role was no longer required.

And with that, the flashiest Ford of the early Fifties disappeared. But, selling more than 17,000 units in 1950, it had already done its job – beating company expectations and buying time.

Ford's 1950 flathead V-8 picked up refinements like new pistons, a new camshaft and a three-blade fan that replaced the four-blade version.

Two-toning with a contrasting color cove was used to good effect on the Crestliners with this version in Sportsman Green and Black.

◄ *Kaiser's Traveler led a secret life. From the outside, it looked like a standard sedan. But the rear compartment opened hatchback style, a concept that was ahead of it times.*

SOMETIMES, timing really *is* everything. Take the Kaiser Traveler. Here was a car that thought it was a truck and also a hatchback, before we knew what a hatchback was. The claim to fame for Traveler (along with its upscale line mate, the Vagabond) was a relentlessly sensible design that combined sedan and station wagon.

With a sticker price of $2,088, Traveler was billed as, "The world's most useful car." The idea for Traveler came right from the top. Chairman Henry J. Kaiser had a vacation home near Lake Tahoe,

and used a station wagon to tool around the grounds, carrying everything in it from people to building supplies. Kaiser found the wagon to be a poor compromise – uncomfortable for passengers, and inadequate for hauling cargo. In the summer of 1948, the boss decided that his company should build something better. The result made its production debut in 1949.

The beauty of the Traveler was its flexibility. It was a six-passenger sedan that could be reconfigured in a matter of moments into a utility car, with a big

If you saw the buffalo logo in 1950, ▸
you knew the car was a Kaiser.

The Traveler's interior ▸
was intentionally
utilitarian and rugged
but still looked good.

appetite for cargo. Toting a full complement of people on board, Traveler could also hold 78 cubic feet of gear in back. That number could expand to as much as 130 cubic feet, if only the front seat was used for passengers. The rear deck opened clamshell style, and the back seat folded flush or could be removed completely.

The idea was simple but the execution was not. Over 200 changes were made to a standard Kaiser sedan to turn it into a Traveler. The toughest part of the process was mental, not mechanical. As Kaiser's Manager of Styling, Herbert Weissinger, put it, "You know, our hardest job on the utility car was in overcoming the feeling that it couldn't be done."

Unconventional thinking produced the Traveler, but it was an idea ahead of its time. Though the design worked as advertised, only 21,000 sold in its two-year run from 1949 through 1950. Fifty years later, hatchbacks and SUVs would become popular worldwide. Traveler was no *time* traveler, though. Neither the car nor the company would live long enough to see that day.

◄ *The power under the Traveler hood was the 226.2cid, 100-hp L-head six.*

◄ *The Kaiser Traveler seemed almost full-size in this 1950 magazine ad.*

# Studebaker Commander Starlight Coupe

◄ *The Starlight Coupe had a sweeping, panoramic view.*

IGNORING IT WAS NOT AN OPTION. "It," in this case, was the front end styling of Studebaker's 1950 and 1951 lineup. Bob Bourke's airplane inspired, bullet-nose design was an eye-opening facelift on what was by then a three-year-old body style. Though trumpeted as the "Next Look," Ford was already working the spinner snout styling side of the street. Still, it's the buyers' votes that count, registered with their feet or with their wallets, and a record number of them elected to take a 1950 Studebaker home with them. With well over 300,000 sales, it was Studebaker's best year ever.

Careful study of Studebaker's 1951 styling suggests that the company (or car buyers) thought the 1950 car's nose was a bit too notable. The outer ring of the bullet was now painted body color, instead of chromed. The '51 models may have been toned down a bit, but they were far from subdued, thanks to some modernized mechanicals. Commander models were (along with the Land Cruisers) the first Studebakers to boast an overhead valve, 120-hp V-8 engine. The eight, along with the "Automatic Drive" transmission introduced by Studebaker midway through the 1950 model year, put the South Bend independent on the same page, innovation-wise, with Detroit's Big Three.

The 1951 Commanders ▶ sported V-8s only. The sixes were now found under the hoods of the entry level Studebaker Champions.

Both entry level Champion and upscale Commander series shared the same 115-inch wheelbase platform. Included in the lineup of both ranges once again were two-door models with an elegant, wraparound rear window and an evocative name – the Starlight Coupes. Leaner, and packing 18 more horsepower than the previous year, Commanders like our featured car commanded a little more attention in the burgeoning days of the industry-wide horsepower wars. Top speed was estimated at about 100 mph, and the trip from 0-60 took a little under 13 seconds. Still, economy figures showed that Studebaker hadn't forgotten how to be frugal with a pint of petrol. In the 1951 Mobilgas Economy Run, the Studebaker Commander was a class winner. A three-speed with overdrive model averaged 28 miles per gallon—a figure that many car buyers wish they could match more than 50 years later.

▲ *Passengers were virtually surrounded by glass in the 1951 Commander Starlight Coupe.*

◄ *The 1951 Studebaker interior was cozy in a year when 124,329 Commanders found buyers, up from 69,560 in 1950.*

# Lincoln Capri

◄ *Lincoln's hardscrabble road race success seemed at odds with the upscale, top-down Capri profile.*

EVER HEARD THE SONG, "Hot Rod Lincoln?" Most people would associate Lincoln with luxury – not with being "hot," but it wasn't always so.

In 1950, Cadillac—the self proclaimed "Standard of the World" – entered a car in the famous road race at LeMans, and placed 10th! These improbable racing results added another feather in Cadillac's cap – as if one was needed. By 1952, they held an enormous, 80 percent share of the luxury market.

Rivals like Lincoln sought any opportunity to put a dent in Cadillac's massive hold on this segment. Like Cadillac, they went racing, seeking to link

success on the circuit to showroom sales. "Win on Sunday, sell on Monday" the saying goes, and Lincoln's forays in this arena came not at legendary LeMans, but on the grueling terrain of the Mexican Road Race. Modified, V-8- packing Lincolns led a massive, American assault on the 1952 Carrera Panamericana. Lincoln swept the top four spots in the American stock category, a feat they repeated again one year later.

Meanwhile, back in the showroom, buyers who may or may not have heard of these exploits could wrap some of that V-8 performance in a decidedly more civilized package. The 1952 lineup stretched from the Cosmopolitan to the Capri; the latter

Sales of 27,271 units ▶
placed Lincoln in 19th place
industry-wide in 1952.

offered in two-door hardtop, four-door sedan or convertible models, like this one.

The "drop top" was the priciest in the Lincoln lineup. In a year when the median income for an American family was $3,900, a Capri convertible listed for $3,699, and 1,191 were sold. The '52 Lincoln offered distinctive and understated styling as well as cutting edge mechanicals. Under the sleek skin, Lincoln boasted a new ball-joint front suspension and upgraded drum brakes–the better to keep up with the also-new overhead-valve V-8. De-tuned from race versions, the 317.5-cubic-inch motor yielded 160 hp in street trim, and was linked to a Hydra-Matic transmission—a dual range automatic built, interestingly enough, by GM.

The combination of new power and clean lines went over well with luxury buyers in 1952. Lincoln never threatened almighty Cadillac for sales supremacy, but the Mexican race success put a shot of "south-of-the-border spice" into the company's bottom line.

▼ *The new 160-hp V-8 was Lincoln's first overhead-valve engine.*

▲ *The interior invited drivers and passengers to enjoy the top-line Capri touches.*

**1952 Lincoln Capri** | 25

◄ *The Muntz Jet, based on the Kurtis Sport, swapped aluminum for a steel body.*

T HE STORY sounds like a headline from the *National Inquirer*: "Madman builds Jets in suburban Illinois."

The "Madman" was one Earl Muntz and his nickname was gained from a bustling career in the 1950s, first as a radio/TV manufacturer and then an over-the-top California car dealer. The Jet was the Muntz Jet—a convertible sports car. The suburbs in question were in Evanston, Illinois, hometown of Muntz and eventually home to the Jet

production facilities. But, the roots of the car, like the manufacturer, traced back to the "golden state." Another Californian, noted race car builder Frank Kurtis, created the forerunner to the Muntz Jet. Known as the Kurtis Sport, it was an innovative, two-seat convertible, with a bathtub-style body made mostly of aluminum. Kurtis Sports could be had in any form from kits to complete cars, and most were powered by flathead Ford V-8s. Kurtis produced about three-dozen cars before selling the company to Muntz for a reported $200,000.

◄ *The 1952 Muntz Jet was 400 lbs. heavier than the car it was based on, the Kurtis Sport.*

*A full set of gauges and the engine-turned dash gave the Jet a sporty look inside.*

*The factory was portrayed along with the famed "Mad Man" Muntz logo.*

Muntz set about making the Jet a little more mainstream. Creature comforts were added (like a Muntz radio), though side curtains were still used instead of roll-up windows. Stretching the wheelbase 13 inches allowed enough room for a back seat. A bolt-on hard top was included, in addition to the canvas soft top. The aluminum body shell was replaced with sturdier steel. Inside, as before, flat, sofa-thick bucket seats faced a full complement of gauges. The car was now more comfortable, but larger and heavier, too. Muntz specified a Cadillac 331-cid V-8 under hood, so performance could keep pace with the added heft.

Muntz built about 28 cars in the original, SoCal plant before pulling up stakes and moving the manufacturing operation to Illinois. More tinkering followed, and more sales, but the Jet never really took flight. The design required massive amounts of hand finishing, the cost of which ultimately grounded the effort. Even at a sticker price of $5,500, Muntz estimated that he was losing $1,000 per car.

When losses crested $400,000, he shuttered the operation and returned to his roots, making and selling televisions and radios. After total production of a few hundred cars (estimates vary from as little as 198 to as many as 490), the Jet passed into automotive lore: another interesting, innovative independent that lived and died in the 1950s.

◄ *Some Muntz Jets were powered by a 331-cid Cadillac V-8 like this one. Others ran with Lincoln V-8s.*

▼ *The Muntz Jet was built with safety in mind.*

# 1953 Buick Skylark

The Buick Skylark was sleek and low-slung by early 1950s standards.

SKYLARK WAS one of a trio of halo cars from General Motors' class of 1953. Three limited production convertibles were introduced that year: the Cadillac Eldorado, Oldsmobile Fiesta and the Buick Skylark. The Skylark was the sportiest looking of the lot and, at $5,000, the least expensive.

Skylark had a semi-custom look, the product of GM Design Director Harley Earl and Buick Styling Chief Ned Nickles. For the occasion, the stylists had temporarily declared Buick front fenders a "porthole-free zone." The windshield was chopped a full four inches, for a more rakish profile. The side view was low and dashing. Fully-radiused wheel wells showcased Kelsey-Hayes wire wheels. In between, a checkmark-styled side molding dove to a dramatic dip just ahead of the rear tires.

Inside, Skylark was full-boat loaded. Two tone, full leather upholstery provided the seating and there were power assists for just about everything (steering, brakes, windows, antenna, seat and convertible top). Under the hood was Buick's first modern V-8. The 322-cubic-inch "Fireball" pumped out 188 hp, 300 lbs.-ft. of torque, and made the trip from 0 to 60 in 12 seconds.

Of the Big Three's big three image cars for '53, only Eldorado would survive the decade. That outcome wouldn't have been predicted in 1953, though. Skylark's 1,690 first year sales were

The arched wheel wells and chopped windshield enhanced the 1953 Skylark's looks.

*The Buick Skylark boasted a ▶ posh cabin with two-tone leather upholstery and power everything.*

### Its beauty is just the beginning

THIS joyous thing of exquisite grace is the Skylark— Buick's stunning new luxury sports car.

Yet the gorgeous beauty of this motorcar is just the beginning of the deep excitement.

For it's a Buick. And in any Buick, the real heart-lift you get is from the manner of its going—impeccably smooth, gentle of ride, superbly easy to handle, trigger-quick in response.

Upon the Skylark, we have lavished practically every modern automotive advance— including the world's newest V8 Engine, Twin-Turbine Dynaflow, Power Steering, Power Brakes, hydraulic control of the antenna, windows, top, and front-seat adjustment.

In other Buicks—SPECIAL, SUPER and ROADMASTER— many of these advances are yours either as standard equipment, or as options at moderate extra cost.

But in *all* Buicks—even the low-priced SPECIAL—you get the Buick Million Dollar Ride, Buick room, Buick comfort, Buick Fireball power—the highest horsepower and compression ratios, Series for Series, in all Buick history.

Your Buick dealer is waiting to seat you at the wheel of the car that will do fullest justice to your dreams and your purse. See him this week.

BUICK *Division of* GENERAL MOTORS

*When better automobiles are built Buick will build them*

### THE GREATEST
# BUICK
### IN 50 GREAT YEARS

*The Skylark showed ▶ beauty from all angles in 1953 advertising.*

more than its GM line mates Fiesta and Eldorado combined, which earned it the right to return for 1954.

In this game of mobile, musical chairs, the Olds Fiesta was the first left standing when the notes stopped, departing after 458 were produced. 1954 proved to be Skylark's last stand and it was retired after 836 were built. The fall from grace had less to do with Skylark's drop in class than it did Eldorado's drop in price.

When the classy Caddy returned for 1954, it was boasting a bottom line of $5,738. Though still expensive by normal car standards (a Chevy 150 series two-door sedan stickered for $1,623) it was fully $2,012 less than the '53 Eldorado, and just $1,383 more than Skylark. At that point, the gap between the Buick and the Cadillac was just small enough that many high-end buyers felt it was worth bridging to buy the Eldo. The Cadillac rang up 2,150 sales and the curtain rang down on the elegant Skylark.

▲ Handsome Kelsey-Hayes
chrome wire wheels were
dressy and sporty.

◄ The famed Buick "Fireball"
322-cid, 188-hp straight
eight was the Skylark's
power plant.

# Chevy Corvette

*◄ From the tail sprang a pair of modest fins, and the convertible top stowed flush under a hard boot for a clean appearance.*

IF NECESSITY IS THE MOTHER OF INVENTION, then the parts bin must be dear ol' dad.

It was from this happy marriage that Corvette sprang–the low and sporty little Chevy that would go on to become America's Sports Car. The two seater that made its début in 1953 bears little resemblance to the techno-marvel that currently rules the Chevy roost. The first Corvette was done on a strict budget and short timeframe. Built on a chopped version of Chevy's passenger car chassis, the engine was a worked version of the venerable "Blue Flame Six." The resulting 150-hp motor over-matched any manual transmission that the General

had in its arsenal, so Corvette was available only with a two-speed, Powerglide automatic.

Up front, the 'Vette had a wide mouth grille flanked by laid-back lights. The headlamps were recessed behind sporty, mesh stone guards. From the tail sprang a pair of modest fins, and the convertible top stowed flush under a hard boot for a clean appearance. The side view showed a restrained use of trim – unusual for the day – and a tasteful, wraparound windshield. Less successful was the side glass, which wasn't glass at all. Rather, a set of plastic side curtains took the place of roll-up windows. This allowed a whole new generation of Americans the opportunity to find out what

*The far-flung gauges used ▶ in the Corvette weren't easy to read at speed.*

*The AC Spark Plug company ▼ proudly shared space with the new Corvette in this 1953 ad.*

European sports car owners had been swearing at for all those years.

Use of fiberglass for Corvette's body was innovative, but resulted in production headaches. The Molded Fiber Glass Company supplied the 46-piece bodies to Chevrolet. Assembly proved complicated and slow, and ultimately, just 300 1953 Corvettes were produced. Most were promised to VIPs and all were painted the identical shade of Polo White.

Though a good handler, the first Corvette was underpowered and rough around the edges – more notable for what it would become than what it was. And it almost *wasn't*, after 1953. Chevy built 3,640 Corvettes for 1954, and about 40 percent were left unsold at year's end.

The imminent arrival of Thunderbird from cross-town rival Ford gave Corvette a stay of execution. GM also added what was needed from the start – more horsepower and a stick shift. Though 1955 production was a woeful 700 units, Corvette turned the corner that year, its sales gained traction and the ranks of the fiberglass faithful have been expanding ever since.

▲ The Corvettes got plenty of hands-on attention in 1953 as the assembly process was refined.

◄ The first Corvettes were powered by the famous Chevrolet "Blue Flame Six."

# 1953 Kaiser Dragon

◄ Kaiser's "widow's peak" roofline was accentuated by exotic "Bambu" vinyl covering. Chrome wire wheels were optional.

THOUGH INTRODUCED on Halloween day, 1952, the 1953 Kaiser Dragon was far more treat than trick.

The Dragon was offered only as a four-door sedan, lavishly equipped and impressively priced at $3,924 – almost 70 percent more than the least expensive model in Kaiser's lineup.  Dragons were easy to spot on the street. Kaiser's rounded hardtop-style roofline was accented with a padded "Bambu" vinyl top. Hood ornament and fender script were plated in 14-carat gold.  Dressy, chrome wire wheels were

optional, but wide whitewalls were standard.

With gilded trim and padded roof, Dragons were undeniably dressy outside, but what made them unique was what you found behind closed doors. The Kaiser Dragon was one of the first automobiles so well appointed that it was bought from the inside out.

A designer named Carlton Spencer is credited for taking car cabins beyond the subdued hues of the day. Spencer's fabrics and eye-opening color

The Dragon's interior was truly sumptuous. Ultra rare "Laguna" cloth interior (seen here) was the product of an outside design consultant.

A color magazine ad from 1953 promoted the Kaiser car line.

combinations first appeared in Kaiser products in the early Fifties. By 1953, the Dragon was a stand-alone series, with stand out style inside. One rare combination coupled more "Bambu" vinyl with "Laguna" cloth seat fabric (designed by fashion consultant Marie Nichols and seen in this fine '53). Below, passengers could sink their toes into plush, shag carpeting. Finishing the interior were a full complement of standard features like power steering, a radio with rear speaker, heater, defroster, tinted glass, electric clock, a backlight shade, Hydra-Matic transmission (sourced from GM) – and even carpeting in the trunk. A personalized nameplate (also gold) adorned the glove box, a testimony to the owner's good taste.

The 118-hp straight-six engine had to make do with an extra 200 lbs. of weight in the Dragons, thanks to added sound insulation. This pushed the car's curb weight over 3,300 lbs., and 0 to 60 was clocked in a rather unhurried 15 seconds. Clearly, these Dragons weren't built for *draggin'*. Amidst all that luxury inside, though, it's doubtful that anyone ever noticed.

Kaiser Dragons were rarely seen then and aren't seen very often now. It is estimated that just 1,277 were built in 1953.

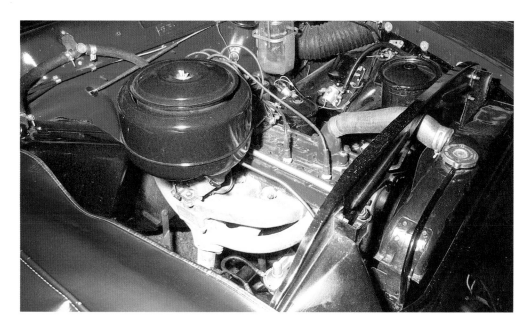

◄ *The 118-hp six-cylinder engine powered a car that weighed in at 3,300 lbs, due in part to its added sound insulation.*

▼ *When Kaiser decided to dress up its 1953 design, its Dragon was the fashionable result.*

◄ The Nash Healey was one of the cross-cultural collaborations of the 1950s.

AS THE STORY GOES, Donald Healey met George Mason during a transatlantic crossing onboard the Queen Elizabeth in 1949. Healey, then a well-known British sports car driver and builder, was en route to Cadillac to see if he could persuade the company to sell him some of their new OHV V-8s for a sports car project that he was designing.

During their impromptu, oceanic chat, Healey told Mason (President of Nash-Kelvinator) of his upcoming trip to GM. Seeing an opportunity to air out Nash's musty reputation, Mason offered him the option of buying the Nash Ambassador's OHV inline six. Healey declined – at first. The idea of a Cadillac V-8 stuffed into a British two-seater was a concept whose time was about to come.

When it did, though, it was in an Allard, not a Healey. Cadillac turned him down cold. Undaunted, Healey took Mason up on his offer and plans soon began for a marriage of Healey's Silverstone roadster with the Nash straight six. The first of the British-built, aluminum-bodied sports cars emerged with a front grille lifted from the 1951 Nash Airflyte and packing an Ambassador engine. The motor was massaged to the tune of 125 hp thanks to a beefy cam and dual carburetors.

The cars were raced early and often, and they quickly gained respect for their performance, competing with distinction at such fabled venues as the 24 Hours of Lemans. Despite their strong showings, winning on Sunday never really

◄ The lithe body lines of the Nash Healey contrasted sharply with its somber-looking grille.

# NEW NASH STEALS MARCH ON "DREAM CARS"

*Rarely seen in Nash ads, the ▶ Nash Healey helped portray an exotic setting in 1955.*

*Nash Healey's ▶ interior was far from the Spartan sports car basic of the early 1950s.*

translated into selling on Monday. (Total production from 1951 through 1955 was just 506.)

A second-generation car emerged in 1952, with several significant differences. Panelcraft's aluminum bodywork was replaced by a sleek, steel Pininfarina style. Elegant from back and sides, the new look was capped by a rather stern front view, with a stout, oval grille and inboard headlights. There was a bigger motor under the bonnet, with a net gain of 10 hp and 15 lbs.-ft. of torque (now 135 and 230, respectively). Weight was down, but prices were heading up. By 1953, Nash Healey models were carrying a cheeky sticker price of $5,908 – this at a time when Chevy's new Corvette stickered for $3,513, and even Buick's semi-custom Skylark cost $5,000.

Of course, high price and limited production are two ingredients that bode well for a car's future value to collectors. That and the Nash Healey's racing provenance have made these cars highly coveted today.

▲ Rare as these spoked wheels, by the end of its 1951 through 1954 production run, some 506 Nash Healeys had been rolled out to the public.

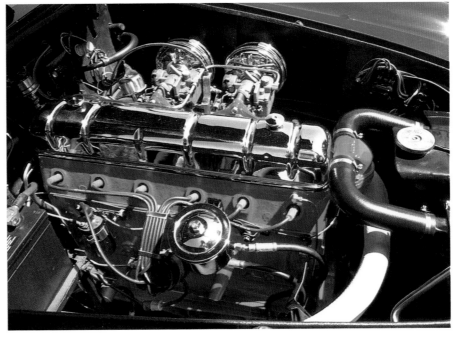

◄ The 253-cid Nash straight-six engine produced 135 horsepower and 230 lbs.-ft. of torque.

# Oldsmobile Fiesta

I N THE LAST YEAR OF A STYLING CYCLE, with all new models just around the corner, GM could've been forgiven if they'd just phoned in their 1953 lineup, and saved the fireworks for 1954. They didn't. Instead, the General mustered a trio of one-off, semi-custom cars to headline the Buick, Cadillac and Oldsmobile lineups.

Oldsmobile's entry in this class of 1953 was called the Fiesta. Based on the big, 98 series convertible, Fiesta (like Buick's Skylark and Cadillac's Eldorado) was notable for the extremes that the company went to, considering its low production potential. Olds designers took a page from the customizer's

book on how to inject some new life into an old body style. Chopping the top and the new, wraparound windshield, they lowered the height of the car by about 3 inches.

While solid colors were available on Fiestas, most wore a flashy, two-tone coat of paint. Hue number two was applied not only to the deck lid but also the rear fender tops. Special chrome trim was added, most notably a strip running north and south down the middle of the trunk. The look was topped off with Fiesta badges, and three bar, spinner hubcaps. Parked inside on two-tone leather seats, the driver faced a dazzling, chrome-laden dashboard that could only have been found in the Fifties.

*The Olds Fiesta had a street-custom look, especially its custom "spinner" wheelcovers.* ▶

*The Oldsmobile Fiesta* ▶
*Convertible was featured in this 1953 A.C. Spark Plug ad.*

The "dual dish" dash featured a pie-plate sized speedometer on the left, balanced by a like-size speaker housing on the right. As befitting its upscale price tag ($5,715), Fiesta was festooned with just about every luxury feature that GM had at its disposal. The most curious of the gadgetry was GM's Autronic Eye—a slightly ominous looking, dash-mounted device that automatically dimmed headlight high beams in response to oncoming traffic. A higher compression ratio allowed the Fiesta's 303.7-cid Rocket V-8 to reach 170 hp – five more than other Olds.

Fiesta went from show car in 1952 to production by mid-'53, a quick entrance matched only by an equally fleet departure. Priced $2,500 more than an Olds 98 convertible, just 458 people put one in their garage. When the 1954 Oldsmobiles arrived, Fiesta was gone from the lineup. Fifty years later, the rest of the Olds lineup followed suit.

◄ *The deck lid chrome strip was distinctive to the 1953 Olds Fiesta.*

▼ *The Olds Rocket V-8 pumped out 210 hp.*

# Packard Caribbean

◄ *The faux hood scoop was unique to the Caribbean but not the broad chrome grille.*

I T WAS A SHOW CAR STUNNER. When it made its debut at the 1952 International Motor Sports Show in New York City, the Packard Pan American dropped jaws and raised eyebrows. In an era when most cars were boxy of body and copiously chromed, the Pan American was neither. Distinctly low slung and cleanly styled, the Pan American was the creation of Designer Richard Arbib. Working from a stock, 250 series convertible, Arbib "channeled" the body, to achieve the daring, low lines.

Packard gave the green light for development, and the task fell to in-house stylist Dick Teague to transform the Pan American into something more production-friendly. Unfortunately, by the early Fifties, Packard was bleeding red ink, and didn't have the capital to properly finance the job. That meant so long to the Pan American's so-low profile. Teague adopted all of the Pan American styling cues that funds would allow.

The new car got a wide hood scoop up front (non-functional, unlike the show car), and a "continental" tire holder in back. Sporty wire wheels showcased by fully radiused wheel wells highlighted the side view.

*Inside, the Packard had room for ▶ six people and featured leather upholstery.*

*By the early 1950s, the once mighty ▼ Packard was troubled, though the exotic Caribbean would convince one otherwise, even more than 50 years later.*

High-waisted but handsome, the new creation was called the Caribbean, and offered only as a convertible, with a power operated top. Inside, where the Pan American had been a single bench three-seater, Caribbean had conventional seating for six with leather upholstery. Mechanically, Caribbean mirrored the standard Packard lineup. A 180-hp, 327-cid straight-eight engine provided the power, linked to either manual or Ultramatic automatic transmission. The suspension was standard issue. Since the car sat higher than the ground-hugging Pan American, it's likely that no one ever described it as they had the show car, described by one auto wag as being able to "hug the road like a lovesick sailor."

At $5,210, Caribbean was priced far less than the $ 7,750 Cadillac Eldorado – the most prominent of the 1953 class of upper-class convertibles. Caribbean handily outsold Eldorado too (750 vs. 532), but not for long. A year later, Eldorado got a little less custom and a lot less pricey, and the ranks of the regal ragtops thinned out considerably. Caribbean hung on longer than most, selling 400 units in 1954, and similar numbers in its final two years of 1955 and '56. These models were the last true reminders of Packard's past elegance.

◄ *Packard stylist Dick Teague translated as much from its show car to showroom model as his shoestring budget would allow.*

◄ *Despite its lofty status, the first-year Caribbean got Packard's smaller, five-main bearing straight eight.*

# Cadillac Eldorado

◄ *The ribbed quarter panel immediately identifies the 1954 Cadillac Eldorado.*

THE SECRET TO SUCCESS is sometimes this simple: make smart decisions in short order. In 1953, Cadillac's Eldorado was one of four new luxury convertibles seeking upscale buyers. Five years later, Eldorado was the only one still standing. Fifty years later, you can still buy an Eldorado, because of some deft decision-making back in 1954.

The first Cadillac Eldorado defined "flagship." With its semi-custom styling, opulent appointments and sky high $7,750 price tag, it was the ultimate aspirational automobile. But, automaking is a business, and Cadillac management thought that "The Gilded One" had the potential to do more

than just sell small volume and pump up the brand's prestige. Just 532 Eldorados trickled off the assembly line and into American garages in 1953. That was more than the Olds Fiesta, but less than Packard's Caribbean, and far less than the Buick Skylark.

Measuring the meager sales response, Cadillac decided that the price was too rich for most people's blood – even the blue-blooded clientele who formed the car's customer base. When the 1954 models emerged, the sticker had been slashed to $5,738. To achieve this price, Cadillac had to drop some of the distinctive (and cost intensive) features of the originals, like the stylish, wasp

◄ *The 1954 Cadillac Eldorado had a presence on the highway and was a classic-looking car as well.*

*With two-toned leather upholstery, the Eldorado's interior was as colorful as it was comfortable.* ▶

WHERE *Pride* IS A DIVIDEND !

It has been said, in song and in verse, that the best things in life are free.

And we must say that we side with this romantic conjecture in at least one small regard. For we know that the finest reward of Cadillac ownership costs you nothing.

We have reference, quite naturally, to that wonderful feeling of pride that comes inevitably to new owners of new Cadillacs. It is, in the truest sense of the word, a dividend for your wisdom in choosing the "car of cars."

Of course, when a motorist takes title to his new possession. But we doubt if ever he is fully prepared for the heart-lifting moments which await him behind the wheel.

There is, for instance, the unforgettable

memory of his first journey home . . . and of the joyous welcome of family and friends.

There is his unending pride and joy in the car's great beauty and performance and mechanical perfection.

There is his deep-felt satisfaction at seeing his family surrounded with Cadillac's great comfort and safety and luxury.

And there is his keen awareness of membership in the world's most distinguished fraternity of new car owners.

Won't you come in soon and let us give you a demonstration "preview" of these remarkable "Cadillac dividends"?

We know you would find it the most enlightening experience of your motoring life—and, for our own part, it would be a pleasure to introduce you to the Standard of the World.

*Cadillac*

YOUR CADILLAC DEALER

*Few words were needed to get the point across that the 1954 Cadillac was a special car.* ▶

waistline and chopped windshield. However, broad, ribbed quarter panel covers were added and Eldorado staples like chrome plated wire wheels, leather interior and a low-rise metal boot for the convertible top carried over. The result was a car that was less custom, but more affordable to more people.

All Cadillacs were restyled for 1954, and the Eldorado was especially easy on the eyes. Underneath the skin, a stiffer frame and revamped suspension got rid of some of the "Cadillac Float." And, while no one would mistake them for sports cars, handling was much improved. The 331-cid V-8 was up 20 horsepower (at 230) though it was lugging 4,815 lbs.

The strategy quadrupled Eldorado production (2,150) and squelched Skylark sales (836). The Buick never recovered and disappeared after 1954. Only Packard's Caribbean remained to duke it out with Eldorado for flagship bragging rights from the Class of '53, and that car's departure (after 1956) was due to bad management, rather than bad product. Eldorado's success began when it "excessed" just enough luxury to keep the price within reach of its buyers.

▲ Rear-end styling for the 1954 Cadillac would change with the Eldorado getting its own look in 1955.

◄ Better breathing boosted horsepower as Cadillac found an extra 20 horses using modified intake manifolds and timing tweaks in the 1954 Eldorados.

# 1954 Hudson Italia

*◄ Despite its exotic looks and European lineage, the Italia never found a market.*

THE HUDSON ITALIA was a curious mix of Italian flair with American flash. Euro-name notwithstanding, the design flowed from an American pen—that of Hudson stylist Frank Spring—and the car was built by Carrozzeria Touring in Milan, Italy. The front view was dominated by a great, gaping egg-crate grille, book ended by headlights that peered from beneath deep cut air scoops (functional, to aid brake cooling). Below sat a dramatic "praying mantis" bumper. The side view was long and dramatically low (about 10 inches lower than other Hudsons), with a thin side spear riding just above the Borrani wire wheels. Out back, both a gracefully sculpted deck lid and fenders were trumped by a trio of recessed, scallop-cut tubes that held tail and backup lights.

Though known to most for its form, the Italia pioneered in function as well. In addition to those brake cooling fender vents, this cross-cultural car featured an industry leading flow-through ventilation system. Air entered the cabin through a cowl vent and exited via vents placed above the back window glass. Else wise inside, Italia boasted anatomical bucket seating for two.  Colorful two-toned leather seats were individually adjustable for a custom fit. Behind the passengers was a large parcel shelf, with tie-down straps to hold luggage. Doors were cut into the roof some 14 inches to aid ingress and egress from the low slung two-door.

*◄ The Italia's rear fender treatment combined dapper Italian design with 1950s America's fascination with all  things that were jet-like.*

*The Hudson Italia present-ed an unforgettable first impression, front or back.*

*The Italia's interior brought to mind a contemporary car like the Mercedes Gull Wing.*

In the early 1950s, many automakers began to recognize the value of having a sporty two-seater as a halo car in their lineup. So, by the middle of the decade, the market had seen the Italia, Corvette, Kaiser-Darrin, Nash Healey and the Ford Thunderbird. Many of these were (or became) high performance models. Not so, Italia. Underneath the striking body was the humble chassis of the Hudson Jet. It didn't matter.

Italia's aluminum body looked fast and exotic, and that was its mission, to point the way towards future Hudson designs. Alas, the future wasn't to be. Hudson only survived through 1957 and the Italia's lifespan was shorter still. Just 26 Italias were produced and sold in 1954 and '55 (25 production cars and a prototype). Dramatic styling, dual citizenship, high price (the dealer's cost was $4,800) and an ultra-low build count assure the Italia a place on the short list of America's rarest and most collectible Fifties cars.

**AUTOMOTIVE FASHIONS: THE HUDSON ITALIA**

WATER COLOR BY LESLIE SAALBURG

The shape of things to come is suggested by Hudson Motor Car Company's Italia. This streamlined closed coupé has a 105-inch wheelbase, is powered by a 114-h.p. Jet engine. The body was designed and produced by Carrozzeria Touring, in Italy, and has a silhouette ten inches lower than standard models. Other innovations are the airscoops and intakes to cool front and rear brakes, the doors carried fourteen inches into the roof, and the triple bank of chrome tubing in the rear, housing tail-, signal, and back-up lights.

◄ *This color ad is almost as rare as the cars it promoted.*

▼ *The humble Hudson inline-six had the lofty moniker: "Special Jet Instant Action Engine with Super Induction."*

# 1954
# Kaiser-Darrin

◄ *The Dutch Darrin design lost some elements from prototype stage but not its puckered grille and unique sliding doors.*

IT WAS LONG, LOW AND SLEEK, and Henry Kaiser didn't like it one bit. The subject of his scorn was a striking two-seater—a prototype sports car built by legendary designer Howard "Dutch" Darrin. Henry Kaiser was his boss, and Mr. K's lack of approval almost put the kibosh on this Kaiser. However, Mrs. K was also in attendance on that fateful day in 1952, and upon seeing Darrin's new creation, she reportedly called it "The most beautiful thing I have ever seen." The boss's boss held sway, and the Kaiser-Darrin was on its way.

Production of the fiberglass two-seaters began in January 1954, in Kaiser's Jackson, Michigan, plant. Along the way from prototype to production, many changes were made to the original concept, to make them easier to manufacture in quantity. Lost in the process were the split windscreen, ultra-low profile and triple carburetion. However, the most distinctive features of Darrin's design – the pursed lips grille and the patented sliding doors – remained intact in the final versions. The three-way landau-style convertible top was also unique. It allowed for an intermediate position that exposed the top, but blocked back drafts.

*The gauges were scattered ▶ across the dashboard on the prototype but were herded together on production models for better visibility.*

*Imagine being the winner of a ▼ Kaiser-Darrin! Cars were popular prizes in 1950s contests.*

Priced at $3,668 (in an era when you could buy a Cadillac for less), the Kaiser-Darrins were high style, but not high performance. That was fixable. More significantly, they were launched just as Kaiser's fortunes were waning. That was terminal. It was as if the most exquisitely styled life preservers were put on deck, but the ship they were on board was the Titanic.

Kaiser sank in 1955. The automaker pulled out of the car business, but before it floundered, Darrin did what he could to salvage his sports car vision. The designer reportedly bought up about 50 of the remaining cars. Fitted with 331-c.i.d. Cadillac V-8's, the final cars helped bring the story full circle. With 300-plus horsepower, the last Kaiser-Darrins were also the best. They fulfilled the style and performance promise made by the prototypes but lost in production – stripped by cost cutting moves.

It's estimated that just 435 were built in all, including this 1954 Yellow Satin beauty.

◄ The Kaiser-Darrin had a dashing style that still looks good after 50 years.

◄ An F-head Willys straight-six engine powered most Kaiser-Darrins, though a few   though a few later  cars packed a beefy Cadillac V-8.

# Chevrolet Bel Air

*◄ Priced at $2,305, 41,292 Bel Air convertibles like this one were sold in the '55 model year.*

IF I HAD TO PICK A FLASHPOINT for cars of the 1950s, this would be it. The lineup that Chevy fielded from 1955 through '57 was the unofficial lightning rod for all things that we remember well about cars of this decade. Two-tone paint, powerful V-8s, styling that stands up to time – they all came together here in a perfect storm that over-swept the car-buying public. Consider that almost one out of every four new cars sold in the U.S. in 1955 was a Chevrolet.

The '55 Chevy shared the same wheelbase as 1954 models, but that was mostly where the resemblance stopped. Bolted into the new, lighter chassis was

a new, small block V-8 engine. The optional 265-cid V-8 weighed less than the six-cylinder engine, yet had over 30 percent more power (162 hp). An available Power Pack (dual exhaust and a 4-barrel carburetor) pushed horsepower up to 180. To many eyes, the first year of the 1955 through 1957 styling trilogy was the finest. The '55s were modern and clean looking, with tasteful two-toning and admirably restrained brightwork—perfect for the tenor of the times.

1956 brought the first freshening, ushered in with a wide, low grille and revamped two-hue paint schemes. The back was little different from '55, save one new design that was destined to confuse

*◄ The perfect completion to the "Hot Ones" trilogy was the stunning 1957 Chevrolet.*

*The 1956 sticker read $2,443* ▶
*and 41,268 Americans put new*
*Bel Airs in their driveways.*

*A new style and a new V-8* ▼
*engine attracted a lot of at-*
*tention and legions of buy-*
*ers to the 1955 Chevrolet.*

## Chevrolet's *red-hot* hill-flatteners!
### 162 H.P. V8 - 180 H.P. V8

See that fine fat mountain yonder?

You can iron it out, flat as a flounder . . . and easy as whistling!

Just point one of Chevrolet's special hill-flatteners at it (either the 162-h.p. "Turbo-Fire V8," or the 180-h.p. "Super Turbo-Fire"*) . . . and pull the trigger!

Barr-r-r-r-o-o-O-O-OOM!

Mister, you got you a flat mountain!

. . . At least it *feels* flat. Because these silk-and-dynamite V8's gobble up the toughest grades you can ladle out. And holler for more. They love to climb, because that's just about the only time the throttle ever comes near the floorboard.

And that's a pity. For here are engines that sing as sweetly as a dynamo . . . built to pour out a torrent of pure, vibrationless power. Big-bore V8's with the shortest stroke in the industry, designed to gulp huge breaths of fresh air and transmute it into blazing acceleration.

You don't have to be an engineer to know that these are the sweetest-running V8's you ever piloted. Just drop in at your Chevrolet dealer's, point the nose at the nearest hill, and feather the throttle open. *These V8's can do their own talking* . . . and nobody argues with them! *Optional at extra cost.*

**SEE YOUR CHEVROLET DEALER**

*motoramic* **CHEVROLET** *Stealing the thunder from the high-priced cars with the most modern V8 on the road!*

gas station attendants for generations to come. The gas cap was hidden behind the driver's side taillight housing. A compression boost bumped up horsepower for both six- and eight-cylinder engines. The straight six rose to 140 hp. V-8s still started at 162 hp, but the option sheet also included hot (a 205-hp Super Turbo-Fire V-8) and hotter (the 225-hp, dual 4-barrel Corvette motor). Softer springs in the 1956 cars made for a smoother ride.

The '57 Chevy may have been the most impressive of all. Competing with all new models from both Ford and Chrysler, Chevy rolled out one last variation of its "Hot Ones." It was a fine design. A mesh cut, split grille was book ended between rubber bumper bullets up front. Along side, a full-length spear spread into a broad, ribbed wedge on the back fenders. Capping off the look was a set of elegant, tall fins, integrated deftly with taillights and bumper. In all, it was the sort of facelift that would have you asking for the name of the plastic surgeon.

The '57 Chevy's distinctive fin and fender treatment became one of the decade's styling icons.

While the Blue Flame six was back and better for 1955, the real news under the hood was the new Turbo Fire V-8, with horsepower ranging from 162 to 180.

*Restyled just enough to look new and different was the 1956 Bel Air convertible.* ▶

*"Hide and seek" placement of the gas filler in 1956 Chevys would befuddle generations of gas pump jockeys.* ▼

Mechanically, the '57 showed the benefits of three years of sorting and refining. Engineers had stiffened up the chassis and revamped the front and back suspension. Rolling in the revised platform in cars with Powerglide transmission was a larger Chevy small-block V-8. Cars with synchromesh or overdrive still used the "Turbo-Fire 265" as base V-8. the larger new V-8 was bored out to 283 cid and came in six versions offering between 185 and 283 hp. The 250- and 283-hp "Corvette" versions featured a fast (and finicky) Rochester Ramjet fuel-injected system. With the 283-hp option, Chevy became only the second automaker that could boast of one horsepower per cubic inch (Chrysler was first with an optional 355-hp engine for its 300B).

The '57 Chevy lost a battle, but ultimately won the war. In the last year of their styling cycle, Chevy ceded the model year sales crown to rival Ford (though they edged them in calendar year sales and market share). But, the cars from the bow-tie guys went on to become one of the first Fifties Classics—an instant image of the age. The fender and fins of the '57 Chevy are immediately recognizable to thousands of people, even half a century removed.

That new V8 in the '57 Chevrolet is as quiet as a contented cat and as smooth as cream. And it's cat-quick in response when you ask for action!

No household tabby sitting in a sunny window ever purred more softly than Chevy's new V8 engine. It's so kitten-quiet and cream-smooth that you can scarcely even tell when it's idling.

But when you nudge the accelerator, you know it's there, all right! It pours out the kind of velvety action that helps you be a surer, safer driver at all times. Its smooth, right-now response keeps you out of unexpected highway emergencies. And it overpowers steep hills with such ease they seem like level landscape.

New Chevrolet V8 engine options put up to 245* high-compression horsepower under your command. With 283 cubic inches of displacement, this beautifully designed V8

is a new, bigger and better edition of the engines that have put Chevrolet at the top of the performance ladder. It's sassy, sure—but as tame to your touch as a purring pussycat.

Try the smoothest V8 you ever put a toe to, and all the good things that go with it. Like new Turboglide—the first and only triple-turbine automatic drive (an extra-cost option). And Chevy's own special sweet and solid way of going. Stop by your Chevrolet dealer's . . . Chevrolet Division of General Motors, Detroit 2, Michigan.

# Chevy puts the _purr_ in performance!

*275-h.p. V8 also available at extra cost. Also Ramjet fuel injection engines with up to 283 h.p.

Sweet, smooth and sassy! The dashing new Corvette (left) and the Bel Air Sport Coupe with Body by Fisher (above)—two of 20 beautiful new Chevies.

▲ The 1957 Chevrolet was popular when it was new and today is a 1950s automotive icon.

◄ The 1955 Chevrolet interior was all new like its exterior.

# Ford Crown Victoria

◄ *"Sash and flash" marked the 1955 Ford Crown Victoria styling.*

FORD'S MAJOR FACELIFT in 1955 worked a minor miracle. The new Fords emerged at the decade's mid-point fresh and forward looking, and sales soared. Most notably new about the view were the two-tone paint jobs. The chrome, checkmark-shaped side trim was a metallic Mason-Dixon line, separating colors north and south. A first year entry in the flagship Fairlane series took Ford's newfound flash one step further.

The Crown Victoria had a rakish roofline, lower than its line mates, and capped with a sash of chrome that rose from the B-pillar and wrapped over the top. The wide, brightwork-band also served as the back boundary for an optional Plexiglas half-roof. The fixed skylight was tinted green to cut down on solar gain, and added $70 to the Crown Vic's $2,202 sticker price. The sky-side window found few takers. Just 1,999 signed on the dotted line for a 'glas-top Victoria in 1955.

There were two main reasons why sales were weak, both of them green. Despite their green tint, Plexiglas-topped Crown Vics were hotter inside than those with a metal lid. The snap-in sunscreen

◄ *The Crown Victoria's wraparound rooftop band added interest overhead while bold side trim divided the dual hue paint scheme.*

*Horsepower inflation had a trickle ▶ down effect in 1950s automobiles. Ford speed-ometers were bumped to 110 mph in 1954 and were raised again to 120 mph in 1955.*

*Ford advertising proclaimed its ▼ new styling in 1955 magazines.*

"Just look at those long, low, lovely lines!"

"Can't wait to try that Trigger-Torque power!"

"Let's go in and talk to our Ford Dealer right now!"

## Only Ford delivers Trigger-Torque power and Thunderbird styling!

The 1955 Ford—and the '55 Ford alone —brings you the split-second reflexes of Trigger-Torque power...the striking beauty of Thunderbird styling...the smartness and good taste of Luxury Lounge interiors.

Until you sample the vitality of Trigger-Torque performance, you haven't really savored driving. With it, you have at your command more "thrust" at the wheels... split-second answers to your power requests.

Indeed, Trigger-Torque takes the hint from your toe so swiftly, so smoothly, you'll sometimes wonder if it doesn't *think* for you! And all this brings you a feeling of confidence and security when traffic requires agility or passing demands swift response.

Ford matches its extra high-torque "Go" with a bonus of high-fashion beauty. And it comes in all 16 of Ford's distinguished new '55 models. Trim, long fender lines and its

eager, sophisticated "going-places" flair give Ford the years-ahead look that's recognized everywhere.

Inside, you sit in the lap of luxury, surrounded by color-and-fabric combinations of distinctive taste and quality . . . so new you've never seen them before in any *car*.

. . .

*To see the '55 Ford is to want to drive it. Why not do both at your dealer's at once?*

*Treat yourself to a Trigger-Torque Test Drive today!* **'55 Ford**

was only partially effective at snubbing solar gain. Air conditioning was newly available at mid-year, but pricey ($435) and rarely seen. *Greenbacks* were the other issue. The Plexi-top "Vickie" stickered for $ 2,272, or $48 more than the Sunliner convertible. Most buyers decided that a true ragtop beat a fixed, see-through top – especially if you saved a few sawbucks in the process. Almost 50,000 people (49,966) plunked down the required $2,224 to drive home a convertible.

Though the 120 hp straight six was standard, most Fairlanes were fitted with a V-8. The Y-block eight was now bored out to 272 cid, and packed 162 hp—182 with the Power Pack (4-barrel carb and dual exhaust) option. A Thunderbird V-8 was also available. The 292 T-Bird mill mustered 193 hp, linked to a 'three on the tree' manual transmission. The optional Fordomatic transmission was re-designed for '55. Throttle kick-down now got you all the way to low gear, for "speed trigger" starts.

The steel top Crown Vics fared far better with buyers than 'glas tops, ringing up 33,165 sales in their first year. Those numbers earned the high style coupes a return engagement in the lineup for 1956.

◄ Ford owners could choose from the 272-cid V-8 or the more exciting 292-cid Thunderbird V-8.

# Thunderbird

◄ *The fins in back and subtly restyled front made the 1957 T-Bird a sleek-looking car.*

THESE DAYS, Corvette and Thunderbird are hardly competitors. The Chevy is the premiere American sports car and the Ford is teetering on the brink of extinction. But 50 years ago, it was a different story. Back then, the T-bird and the 'Vette had a rivalry in the same sense that a hammer has a rivalry with a nail. In the three years that they competed head to head in the open two-seater class (1955 to 1957), Thunderbird cleaned house, outselling Corvette by a five-to-one margin (53,166 to 10,506). The competition was short and sweet, breaking up in 1958, when Ford forsook the two-place segment in search of the larger market for larger cars.

The fact is, neither car would exist if it weren't for the other. The main reason why Ford put their two-seat, sporty car into production in 1955 was in response to Corvette, the two-seat sports car introduced in 1953. By 1955, though, Corvette's flaccid sales had Chevy contemplating pulling the plug on the fiberglass flier. Enter T-Bird. The imminent arrival from their cross-town rival ensured that Corvette would live to fight another day.

The popularity of the early (1955 through 1957) "Birds" isn't hard to understand. Beneath the lithe lines of the beautifully proportioned body was a 292-cid V-8, while above was a power convertible

◄ *The 1956 Thunderbird was on the upscale side of the Corvette and rang up 16,155 sales compared to just 700 Chevy Corvettes.*

*The porthole windows have long* ▶ *been considerd a styling staple of early Thunderbirds and were an additional option on the optional hardtops.*

*Ford's 1957 ad series* ▼ *"Adventures in Motion" combined Ford and Mercury products.*

SETTING THE PACE ON THE AMERICAN ROAD

Adventures in motion:
the Ford Family of Fine Cars

FORD · THUNDERBIRD
MERCURY · LINCOLN · CONTINENTAL

• Brand-new line-up of V-8 engines
• New way to smother bumps
• New cornering ... new automatic controls ... new non-slip feature.

Take a front seat at any of the Ford Motor Company test tracks and one fact is clear: Ford, Mercury, Lincoln, Thunderbird or Continental all have the talent for quick starting, get-away snap, cornering ease and riding comfort. As we've been saying—they set the pace on the American Road. The big edge in performance grew out of young-mindedness—deliberately building cars that are ahead in everything that makes a car go. Examples follow:

top (or removable hard top). Ford touted Thunderbird as a "personal" car, not a sports car, and the $2,944 T-Bird was a study in contrasts with the ostensibly similar, $2,934 Corvette. The body was steel (vs. Corvette's fiberglass), the windows rolled up (Corvette had plastic side curtains), and the tops were snug fitting (not so much in Corvette).

1956 brought refinements outside and inside. An optional 312-cid V-8 joined the 292, and a softer sprung suspension smoothed out the ride. Flip out side vents were added to the front fenders, to boost interior ventilation. The year saw the addition of two keys to T-Bird fashion, both borne out of function. Porthole windows were fitted to the C-pillars on optional hard tops (the better to see to what was along side). And, the spare tire was relocated from the trunk to the rear bumper—to increase Thunderbird's appetite for luggage.

Thunderbird swung into its third year with a stunning restyle, arguably the cleanest of the trilogy. The '57's front end was freshened, bumper

▲ The 1957 Thunderbird species was quite distinct from its early "birds of a feather."

◄ The 1956 interior continued the clean and cozy look begun in 1955.

*The 1955 Thunderbird interior was ▶ all business and still offered a taste of luxury.*

*A Thunderbird rally is the scene in ▼ this 1956 Ford ad for "America's exciting new car."*

THE SATURDAY EVENING POST

*Hard top, soft top or open—the Thunderbird is the star in any setting!*

And now: the latest version

of America's most exciting car:

Ford THUNDERBIRD for '56

**Ready to give you a new lease on driving fun, this newest version of America's favorite dream car is more stunning in style . . . more thrilling in power . . . more luxurious in comfort.**

Here, poised for flight you see what many people hardly dreamed possible: a more beautiful, more powerful, more distinctive Thunderbird.

The graceful contours of its long, low lines . . . the unique flair of its new spare-tire mounting . . . the dazzling sheen of its new two-tone colors are but a hint of its newness.

It is when you put the selector in drive position and nudge the gas pedal of a Fordomatic model

that the new Thunderbird will really take you by the heart. Nestled beneath that sleek hood lies a new 225-h.p. Thunderbird Y-8, ready to revise all your ideas of how a car should respond.

Now, you may choose hard top, soft top or both. There's a glass-fibre hard top and a foldaway fabric top. Now, the interiors are richer—more beautiful than ever. Now, you get the added protection of Ford's exclusive Lifeguard design. Now, the ride is smoother—the cornering is flatter than ever. And, as always, you may have optional power steering, brakes, windows and seat. Ask your Ford Dealer just how soon *you* can start enjoying the better things of driving.

*The 1956 Thunderbird's brand-new rear spare-tire mounting folds back handily, as quick as a wink. It adds as greatly to your luggage space as it does to the over-all beauty of the car.*

bullets removed, and grille reworked. In back, more changes: a longer rear deck, revamped bumper and a set of small, angled tailfins sprouted from the fenders. T-Bird's engine choices expanded dramatically, now including both dual four barrel and supercharged versions of the 312-cid V-8.

Thunderbird did everything that was asked of it, providing a classy, sporty, flagship for the line and a Corvette killer in the showroom, but Ford wanted more. More sales, specifically, which they knew could only be found in a bigger car with a back seat. So, even as it launched to critical acclaim and sales success, the little Birds were on the endangered species list. Ford was already designing a four-seat replacement for the 1958 model year, after the three-year cycle had run its course.

But, that was a future known only to Ford insiders. In 1955, '56 and '57, T-Bird was as cool as it got: an instant classic and one of the first of the era to be seen as a symbol of the Fifties. And 45 years later, when Ford reintroduced the Thunderbird to its lineup, these were the cars they reached back to for inspiration.

◄ Unlike some open-top cars, Ford's Thunderbird looked stylish with its optional top in place.

◄ The famous Thunderbird porthole windows first appeared on the 1956 models.

▲ The V-8 offered 193 available horses in the introductory 1955 Thunderbird.

*Everyone knew the Thunderbird had* ▶
*power and the V-8 logo added to the*
*mystique.*

*A 340-hp V-8 was available under the* ▼
*Thunderbird's hood in 1957.*

The Thunderbird is now available in 5 colors!

# 6 a.m. THUNDERBIRD time

Doctor, Lawyer, Merchant, Chief—no matter who you are—you'll find yourself getting up early when your garage is home to a Thunderbird. For here is a truly delightful package of sheer pleasure—all the way from its "let's go" look to the "let's go" performance of its Thunderbird Special Y-block V-8.

What's more—that comfortable seat is nearly *five* feet wide and it's power-operated. The steering wheel is still another comfort feature —adjust it in or out, as *you* like it.

As for weather—your Thunderbird can have an easily demountable hard top *and/or* a snug fabric top. Windows roll up . . . power-operated if you like. Power steering, power brakes, Overdrive and Speed-Trigger Fordomatic are also available. These are important details, but the main thing is the low and mighty car itself! Why don't you obey that urge and try one today. Your Ford Dealer is the man to see.

This is the Thunderbird Special Y-block V-8 4-barrel carburetor, 8.5 to 1 compression ratio, 198-h.p. with Fordomatic . . . try it!

An exciting original by **FORD**

◄ *Pontiac's Safari shared many of the Chevy Nomad's spiffy styling cues like the s-shaped B-pillars.*

THE PONTIAC SAFARI might have arrived about 50 years too soon. Today, we think nothing of driving pickup trucks for personal transport. And the only time most SUVs ever venture off-road is when the driver misjudges a u-turn and plows through a neighbor's petunias. But, back in the Fifties, roles were more traditional – for people and cars. Station wagons were the vehicle of choice for family transport. Straight forward as a pair of sensible shoes, station wagons offered comfortable passage for people and their belongings. "Sporty" really wasn't part of the station wagon lexicon, which is why the Safari (and its corporate cousin, the Chevy Nomad) opened so many eyes when they arrived in 1955.

In GM's brand family, Pontiac was positioned upscale from Chevy. So too, the Safari was parked north of Nomad. Priced at $2,962, the Pontiac cost $490 more than the Chevrolet. Indeed, Safari was Pontiac's most expensive model. Befitting its price tag, the Safari had a standard V-8 under the hood. Pontiac's 287.2-cid, 180-hp eight was coupled to a Hydra-Matic automatic transmission. The inside was posh with the upholstery swaddled in two-tone leather and the cargo bay carpeted – a sure sign that this wasn't a workaday wagon.

Rolling on the Chieftain wagon platform, Safari's style was part Nomad and part Pontiac. Both of GM's tony, two-door wagons shared the trick-looking, forward arching B-pillars and the ribbed

*While the Pontiac Safari and ▶ Chevrolet Nomad were similar, the Safari was 7-inches longer.*

*The Safari had a recessed, ▶ ribbed rooftop and chrome tailgate slates.*

rooftop. Safari also wore brightwork ribbons on the hood and rear fender-tops that marked all '55 Pontiacs. Seven chrome slats ran vertically down the tailgate, a la Nomad. Wraparound glass fore and aft and top-level Star Chief Custom trim made for an uncommonly handsome wagon—rakish for its day.

Cars like Safari were early shots across the bow of auto conformity: testing the waters for less rigidly defined roles in all types of transport. These rebels are rare, too. Safari production for 1955 through 1957 ran 3,760, 4,042 and 1,292, respectively. This scarcity and their premium pricing have made these Pontiacs Milestone cars, and has sent many modern collectors on personal safaris to find a Safari.

▲ The cushy, carpeted cargo compartment was a tipoff that Pontiac's Safari wasn't intended to be a working wagon.

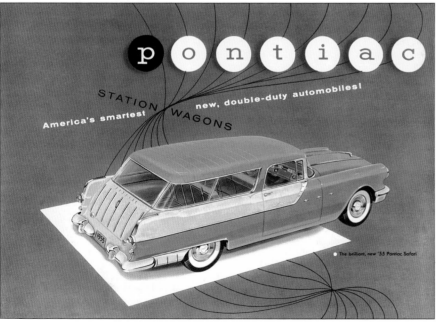

◄ The cover of the 1955 Pontiac station wagon brochure shows the "brilliant" Safari.

# *1955*
# *Studebaker President Speedster*

◄ *The 1955 Studebaker President Speedster continued to exhibit the rakish styling introduced in 1953.*

S OMETIMES, IT'S A SHORT TRIP from
show car to showroom. Case in point: the
1955 Studebaker President Speedster. Twenty
Speedsters were produced for the annual car
show circuit in 1955, and when Studebaker
noticed the strong public response, the car's
popularity lead straight to production. The
brass in South Bend, Indiana, gave the green
light, and a limited run of Speedsters made
their way into the lineup the same year.

First impressions about the Speedster had mostly
to do with the wild, multi-tone paint job, like the
Lemon/Lime treatment on our featured car. The
platform of bold colors and liberal amounts of

chrome insured that all parties casting votes for
*these* Presidents were registered extroverts.

The Speedster was based on Studebaker's elegant
coupe designs of 1953 and '54. These low, clean
and unadorned two-doors were years ahead of
the competition, style-wise. For 1955, Studebaker
reworked (some said *overworked*) the Euro-look for
Speedster, "Americanizing" it with bold two-toning
and plenty of brightwork. The shiny stuff started
with a beefy chrome front bumper with integrated
fog lamps. A sash over the rear roofline was added,
as was polished trim on sides, hood and fender
tops. The final touch was a set of wide whitewall
tires, wrapped around wire wheel covers.

◄ *Originally, the 1955 Studebaker Speedster was to have been painted a body color with a mesh grille. Chrome-loving management added a heavy-handed front end treatment.*

*Speedster's cabin was both colorful and comfortably equipped.* ▶

*Studebaker's cars* ▶
*were well-designed*
*alternatives in the*
*1955 North American*
*automotive market-*
*place.*

The interior was color-keyed to the exterior, with quilted, thickly padded leather and vinyl. The driver's view took in a sporty, engine-turned dash, housing a full complement of gauges.

A 259-cid, 185-hp V-8 was assigned the task of seeing to it that the Speedster lived up to its name. Linked to a three-speed manual transmission or automatic, the fleet coupe could hit a top speed of 110 mph, and run from 0 to 60 in 10.2 seconds.

The Speedster served notice that Studebaker intended to compete with the Big Three in the suddenly splashy world of post 1955 automobiles. It bridged the gap between the elegant, minimalist designs of 1953 and '54 and the bolder stylings of the late 1950s. The party-colored President served a term of just one year, selling 2,215 units at a price of $3,346 each. Then, the torch was passed to the Studebaker Hawks – a series of low-slung coupes that were built from 1956 through 1964.

◄ The Speedster served notice that Studebaker intended to compete with the Big Three in the suddenly splashy world of post 1955 automobiles.

▲ The logo suggested V-8 speed and sportiness for drivers of the 1955 President Speedster.

◄ The Passmaster V-8 pushed the 3,341 lb. Speedster down the road smartly. The trip from 0 to 60 took approximately 10 seconds.

# 1956 Buick Century

◀ *The 1956 Buick Century was considered the "gentleman's hot rod."*

WE THINK OF MUSCLE CARS as being creations of the Sixties, but in a broader sense, the idea of putting a bigger motor in a smaller car had been around for years before that decade of Detroit thunder.

One of the Fifties' finest examples was found in the Buick Century. The Century name traces back to the 1930s, when Buick used it to highlight the triple digit top speed of the new series. The bigger-smaller combo reappeared under the Century banner in 1954. Buick used the mid-size, Special series body and its shorter, 122-inch wheelbase as

the platform for their executive hot rod. Under the hood was the 322-cid Fireball V-8, as found in the flagship Roadmasters. Over the next few years, against a background of minor body changes, horsepower continued to ramp up. The Fireball yielded 195 hp in 1954, 236 in 1955 and 255 in 1956 – the year of our featured car. Performance was impressive. *Motor Trend* posted a 0 to 60 best of 9.6 seconds for the '56 Century, with a 17.1 second quarter mile, and a top speed of 110.8 mph. *Speed Age* also wrung out a '56 Century. Race driver Sam Hanks logged a 0-60 best of 8.1 and pegged the speedometer at 120 mph (the results

*Centurys were fast but not flashy – an understated, upscale approach to muscle that Buick would continue to cultivate for decades to follow.*

*Buick was a popular choice of drivers looking for performance in 1956.*

suggesting both an itchy finger on the stop watch and an optimistic speedometer). Hanks praised the Century's ease of steering and handling, but the racer found it (like all other production cars) under-shocked and under-braked.

Century in '56 had a clean and classy look. A fine mesh grille was featured up front, centered on a saucer-sized medallion, calling out the year, make and model. The familiar Buick gun sight hood ornament was replaced by a jet-like creation. Along the sides, as in '55, a chrome trim line followed the Buick's beltline, dipping to a checkmark notch just ahead of the rear wheels. The brightwork served to bisect two tone colors, too. Meanwhile, the signature four portholes atop the front fenders were stretched into a teardrop shape.

Centurys were fast but not flashy – an understated, upscale approach to muscle that Buick would continue to cultivate for decades to follow. Scratch the surface of the Gran Sport models of the 1960s and 1980s and you'll find more than a little Century. The names may change, but the formula remains the same.

The standard Century interior was done up in a combination of nylon and Cordaveen.

The Fireball V-8 picked up 19-hp in 1956 compared to 1955 levels.

# *1956*
# *Cadillac Series 62 and Eldorado Biarritz*

◄ *In 1956, Cadillac passed Chrysler for 9th place in the industry thanks to cars like the Series 62 convertible.*

A TALE OF TWO FINS. We've already seen how deft brand management allowed Cadillac's Eldorado to outlive its contemporaries in the class of high-class convertibles. By 1955, Eldorado had GM's flagship ragtop title all to itself. In 1956, Cadillac picked up the pace, expanding the Eldorado line and bumping up the prices on both of its convertible models. The high-line convertible was now known as the Eldorado Biarritz, and was joined by a new hardtop model called the Seville.

Both Series 62 and Eldorado models were built on 1955's strong styling with an elegant facelift. The 1955's wide, egg-crate grille was replaced

with a thinner grid. The Cadillac name—in gold script—angled upward, framed by a set of titanic bumper bullets. Telling the two convertible models apart was a task that grew easier as you headed from north to south along the body. Series 62 cars kept Cadillac's sleek, traditional hood ornament, while Eldorados sported a twin-fin hood topper. Side on, fender skirts and hubcaps distinguished the 62s, while Eldorado's wheel openings were fully radiused and sans skirts—the better to show off the stylish, Sabre-spoke wheels. As in 1955, the back view drew the sharpest distinction. Series 62 cars maintained the classic, kick-up mini-fin that Cadillac had been spinning variations on since

◄ *Shark-like fins and skirtless fender wells quickly let viewers know they were looking at a Cadillac Eldorado.*

During the current year, Cadillac has welcomed a greater number of new owners to its motoring family than ever before in history. There are, we think, two basic reasons for this. To begin with, the *temptation* has never before been as great as it is today. The car is beautiful . . . and luxurious . . . and fine in performance to an unprecedented degree. And, secondly, the facts about Cadillac's practicality have never been more difficult to resist. Why not visit your dealer soon and see for yourself? Once you have, we think you'll be anxious to join that happy group of motorists who are making this their *first* Cadillac year. CADILLAC MOTOR CAR DIVISION • GENERAL MOTORS CORPORATION

*Cadillac*

1948. Eldorado contrasted with sharp, shark-like fender tops that forecast the flood of fins to follow, as the decade progressed.

Series 62 convertibles were now priced at $4,711 and the Eldorado Biarritz $6,501; up $263 and $216 respectively, over 1955 levels. Under the hood, the Cadillac 331-cid V-8 was bored out to 365 cid. In Series 62s it was rated at 285 hp, while a dual 4-barrel version in Eldorado generated 305 hp.

Period ads for the Series 62s traded on traditional marketing themes, like Cadillac cache. In the ad shown here (taken from *National Geographic*), smartly dressed citizens in ball gowns and tuxedos were seen on the steps of Boston's Museum of Art, while the copy spoke of temptation and practicality. Those two words don't normally travel in the same circles, but such is the beauty of advertising, and in any event, statistics don't lie. Cadillac sold 2,150 Eldorado Biarritz and nearly four times as many Series 62 convertible coupes—8,300 in all. Swanky sells!

*In 1956, you knew you had ▲ arrived when you were able to own a Cadillac.*

*The opulent interior of ▶ the 1956 Eldorado.*

◄ *Lurking under the batwing air cleaner were a pair of Carter WCFB carburetors; part of the reason the Eldorado engine hit 305 hp in 1956.*

◄ *Two-tone paint was common in 1956 cars but three-tone schemes in the Chrysler lineup were reserved for the New Yorker St. Regis.*

BEHOLD, the New Yorker St. Regis Hardtop. Here's how the company described the new addition to the 1956 lineup in their sales brochure: "a two door Hardtop of breath-taking beauty, incomparable style and elegance, and capable of a thrilling performance that lives up to its low, road-hugging, fleet and powerful good looks." As fine a line of spin as any penned by Madison Avenue. And that's part of the fun of looking back at the Fifties and its cars. It was hyperbole, without apology. Ads were written as if paid by the adjective. Everything had a descriptor added, so even the most mundane features somehow gained importance.

Chrysler's brakes were PowerSmooth, steering was PowerPilot. Continuing the muscle-up theme under the hood, the 354-cid FirePower Hemi linked to the two-speed PowerFlite transmission. The Super-Scenic wraparound windshield was balanced by the aptly named Clearbac rear window. Outrigger bumper guards on the front end were offset by Twin-Tower taillights, housed in Flight Sweep fins. Inside, you lounged on an interior of Sculptured Brocatelle with Satin Petit Point bolsters, and if you wanted a little music while you pondered that, you could choose from the Electro-Touch Tuner or Music Master radios.

Even the forerunner of the CD player could be found in the Fifties. An under-dash phonograph player was

◄ *Chrome slats riding high on rear fenders were calling cards for the 1956 Chrysler New Yorker cars.*

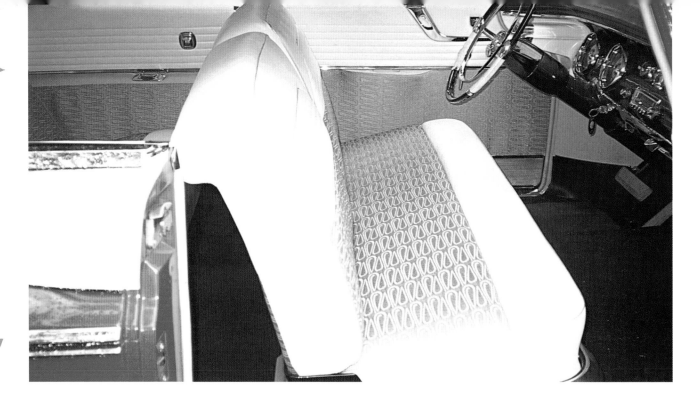

*The 1956 Chrysler had some* ▶
*unusual options including a clock
mounting in the steering wheel
hub and a gasoline-powered
"Instant Heater."*

*In 1956 advertising, the St. Regis* ▼
*and other models were called the
"Power Style Chryslers."*

offered, known, alliteratively enough, as the Hi-Way Hi-Fi. Convenience was the coin of the realm, and Chrysler touted the fact that its new transmission was engaged with the touch of a button. Exactly the same amount of effort was required to open the windows, if you selected the optional, electric lifts.

Decked out in Regimental Red, Cloud White and Raven Black, a '56 St. Regis like our featured car stickered for $3,995 and cut a dashing figure on the road. These PowerStyle cars were an evolutionary step in the Forward Look designs of seminal stylist Virgil Exner. With their long, balanced lines and graceful high-swept fenders, Chrysler's evolving, wedge-like shapes were one year removed from arguably the best looking cars that the decade would produce. But, that's not to overlook fine, rarely seen mid-Fifties Mopars like this one. Driven by a 280 hp Hemi bored out to 354 cubic inches of displacement, models like these earned the reputation of being the best- built Chrysler products of the era. The handsome St. Regis hardtop found 6,686 buyers in 1956.

▲ Burgeoning fins on back of
the New Yorker St. Regis
hinted at things to come at
Chrysler in 1957.

◄ The massive chrome
grille, hood ornament and
prominent logo made it
clear this was a Chrysler.

# 1956 Lincoln Continental Mark II

◄ *Continental was part of a movement by Lincoln to build a car that surpassed segment leader Cadillac in luxury and quality.*

I T WOULD BE EASY to dismiss the Continental Mark II as a luxury car loss leader, but there's more to the story than that. That it lost money seems indisputable. Though priced at the princely sum of $10,400, Lincoln reportedly lost $1,000 on every Mark II they sold. But, if "loss" was true, so too was "leader." The Mark II set the mid-Fifties benchmark for quality control at the luxury level.

Continental was part of a movement by Lincoln to build a car that surpassed segment leader Cadillac in luxury and quality. This would be no small feat

in the Fifties, as Cadillac ruled the upscale domestic ranks and was the self-proclaimed "Standard of the World."

The Mark II's design was the result of a competition pitting outside firms against an in-house entry. In the end, the Ford Special Projects Division rendering won unanimously. The elegant, two-door coupe that ensued was long, fashionably low and beautifully sculpted. Up front was a broad, impressive, crosshatch grille. In back, a bulging spare tire was outlined in the deck lid – a visual nod to the original cars to carry the Continental name,

◄ *The fit and finish of the 1956 Lincoln Continental Mark II were second to none.*

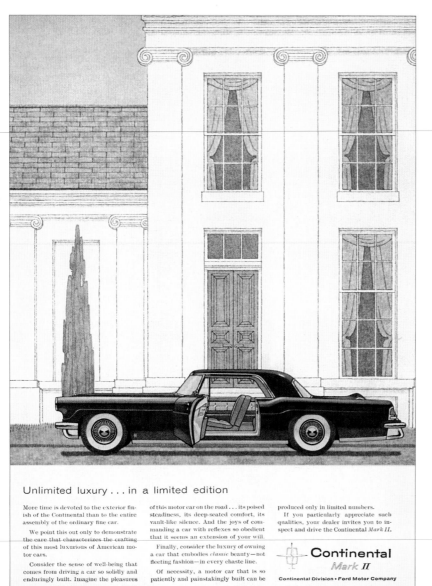

Unlimited luxury . . . in a limited edition

More time is devoted to the exterior finish of the Continental than to the entire assembly of the ordinary fine car.

We point this out only to demonstrate the care that characterizes the crafting of this most luxurious of American motor cars.

Consider the sense of well-being that comes from driving a car so solidly and enduringly built. Imagine the pleasures of this motor car on the road . . . its poised steadiness, its deep-seated comfort, its vault-like silence. And the joys of commanding a car with reflexes so obedient that it seems an extension of your will.

Finally, consider the luxury of owning a car that embodies *classic* beauty—not fleeting fashion—in every chaste line.

Of necessity, a motor car that is so patiently and painstakingly built can be produced only in limited numbers.

If you particularly appreciate such qualities, your dealer invites you to inspect and drive the Continental *Mark II.*

**Continental**
*Mark II*
**Continental Division • Ford Motor Company**

in 1940. A single character crease stretched from end to end, with a kick-up to match the rising rear fender line. The understated, old money appeal was picked up in the car's advertising. A magazine ad trumpeted, "An experience awaits you – the excitement of being conservative." Such was the Continental's presence that when you arrived at a function, the car announced to all that you already had.

Fit and finish were exemplary for its day and assured by considerable individual attention during production. As an example, each Lincoln 368-cid V-8 was balanced before installation. Continental was introduced as a separate division, and a step up from Lincoln. The big coupe was envisioned as the first of a lineup that would grow to include convertible and four-door sedan versions. It wasn't to be.

Seen in the cold light of the accountant's scrutiny, the Mark II's meager sales (2,550 in 1956 and 444 in 1957) didn't justify the costs, and production was discontinued after 1957. Image is important, but sadly, in the case of the Mark II, the bottom line was the bottom line.

▲ Graceful and
distinguished, the
Continental has gained far
more admirers since its
demise than it ever had
when it was alive.

◄ The 368-cid engine used
in the 1956 Continental
produced 285 horsepower.

# 1956 Mercury Montclair Phaeton

◄ *One year removed from 1955's clean-sheet styling, changes were minimal for 1956. The handsome, hooded headlights were a holdover.*

MERCURY WAS ON A ROLL in 1956. Sales of US cars had reached all time highs in '55, and every manufacturer was caught up in the enthusiasm. In 1955, Merc had emerged with a freshening re-style of its 1952 through '54 models. They were fine looking cars, and the longer, lower and wider dimensions undoubtedly had much to do with their market popularity. 1956 brought a modest facelift on 1955: up front, a Big M hood crest rested above the re-styled grille and bumper. In back, "Gel Cap" tail lamps were a new addition. Along the sides, Mercury connected the dots on its brightwork trim. Most models wore a full-length body side

molding that came together in a "Z," just aft of the front doors.

Mercury expanded its lineup from three to four series—the new, budget-priced Medalists slotting in beneath the Custom, Monterey and Montclair lines. The four-door hardtop "Phaetons" were a mid-model year introduction to the lineup. Eventually available in all series, they were notable for their curvy, coupe-like rooflines. The design was so well done that you had to look closely to see that it wasn't a two door. Phaetons graced much of Mercury's print advertising. One magazine ad showed a Montclair Phaeton passing a truck while the copy beneath crowed that, "The Big M's

◄ *The unique, rounded roofline was a distinctive Phaeton design feature and was accented by the dressy, brightwork Montclair-series sash.*

*The open-air atmosphere of the ▶ Phaeton was enhanced by its light and airy interior trim.*

*The top of the line Montclair ▶ Phaetons were the best selling hardtop for Mercury in 1956.*

response is quick as a champion athlete's." Another promoted the giveaway of 80 Phaetons (10 a week) on the Ed Sullivan Show. The combination of four-portal practicality with a hardtop's jaunty looks proved popular with buyers, and Phaeton sales (23,493) were second only to the hardtop (50,562) for bragging rights in the Montclair series.

Under the hood, it was a tale of three motors. The 312-cid "Safety-Surge" V-8 was available with 210 to 235 hp, matched to either a three-speed manual or the mellifluously named Merc-O-Matic automatic transmission. Rare and rarely seen was an optional, high performance 312 with dual 4-barrels making 260 hp.

Not surprisingly, 1956 sales, while good, couldn't keep pace with 1955's torrid levels. Mercury, like other automakers fell back to Earth—the "Big M" settling into seventh place industry-wide.

Announcing a big advance in 4-door hardtops... THE BIG **M** *Phaeton*

Most beautiful 4-door hardtop of them all! Excitingly different styling. Better visibility — with extra viewing area for rear-seat passengers. Easier entrance and exit. See the Big M Phaeton — in the low-silhouette Montclair series. Compare the Phaeton for distinctive styling, visibility, comfort with *any* 4-door hardtop on the market. See why the big move is to THE BIG **MERCURY**

▲ *The Mercury V-8 used in the Montclair Phaeton was enlarged to 312 cubic inches for 1956, up 20-cid from 1955.*

◄ *A fistful of record times at 1956 NASCAR speed trials gave Mercury a lot of "street cred" in the auto industry.*

# 1956
# *Plymouth Fury*

◀ **The public got its first look at the Fury's delta shape at the Chicago Auto Show on January 10, 1956.**

S PEED SELLS. And what better way to speed *sales* for a solid but sleepy lineup of cars, than to add a sporty new model? As we've seen elsewhere in this book, the theory was tried and proven many times in the Fifties, and the '56 Plymouth Fury is one such success story.

To build a Fury, Plymouth began with their mid-size Belvedere 2-door hardtop. The body was shot with a coat of soft, eggshell white paint, set off by gold trim on grille, wheel covers, and the knife-edge, anodized aluminum side spear. Inside, a handsome interior was finished in white, gold and black.

For the firepower, Plymouth reached across the border and plucked the 303 cubic inch V-8 off the shelves of their Canadian cousins. Then, they applied some good 'ol fashioned, American hot-rodding. A hotter, high-lift cam, solid lifters and a boosted (9.25:1) compression ratio netted 240 hp for the 3,650 lb. Fury.

The result was predictably quick: capable of a 0-60 time of 9 seconds flat, with a top speed of 115 to 120 mph in showroom trim. Nice numbers, and with those in hand, Plymouth quickly set out for Daytona Beach, to unchain the Fury. On the beach, the Mopar promptly broke Cadillac's mark for the standing start mile run, with a speed of 82.5 mph, and set a flying

◀ **A gold anodized inlay in the side spear accented the tall thin fins of the 1956 Plymouth Fury.**

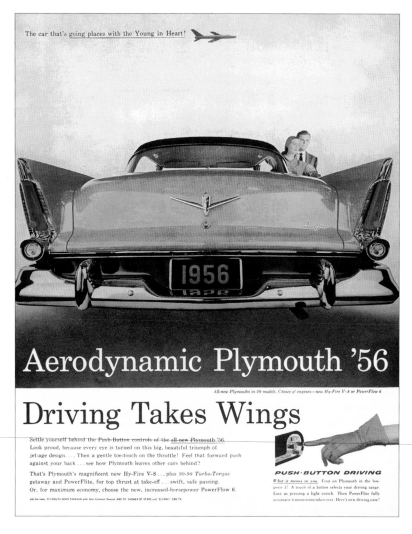

*Plymouth advertising emphasized flight with its "Driving Takes Wings" slant in 1956.*

mile mark of 124.01 mph. Eager to kick sand in the face of the competition, Plymouth looked forward to Daytona Speed Week. Alas, the car hadn't been on sale long enough to qualify for the prestigious events—as a stock entry. Undeterred, Plymouth entered the Fury in the "Experimental" class. A tweaked model posted a jaw dropping top speed of 143 mph on the sand.

Furys rode lower than their line mates, with flatter leaf springs in back and shorter coil springs up front. The suspension modifications made for a firmer riding car, but not enough to loosen your fillings. *Sports Car Illustrated* praised the balance, judging the ride, "not stiff but neither is it soft or mushy."

Fury did its job, injecting some needed flash into Plymouth's family car lineup. For $2,841, you could roll one into your driveway, and in 1956, 4,485 people did just that.

*The dashboard sprouted a tachometer—to keep tabs on the Fury's muscular motor.*

▲ *Plymouth's "Flight Sweep" styling attracted a younger audience with cars like the 1956 Fury.*

◄ *The 303-cid V-8's hot rod hop-ups, like dual four-barrel carbs, domed pistons, a high lift cam and beefed-up suspension, helped Fury live up to its name.*

# Chrysler 300C

IF 1957 WAS THE PEAK of the American automaker's art in the '50s, few would argue that Chrysler was among the first to plant their flag in that high ground. Leading the assault on the pinnacle was the 300C—Chrysler's elegant brute.

The 1957 300 built on past performance and benefited from stunning new styling. In the third year of model production, Virgil Exner's 300C design was dramatic: a long, low, slingshot shape, book-ended by a crisp, trapezoidal grille in front, and soaring tailfins out back. Notably clean and

uncluttered in an era given to excesses, the 300C was – and is – a knockout.

But, looks were only part of the package, and Chrysler's '57 effort produced much to praise on the performance side of the ledger, too. The 392-cid mill made 375 horsepower in standard trim, with an optional 390 hp variant in the wings. Married to a three-speed manual or TorqueFlite push-button automatic, the 300C was hell on wheels. It proved to be the fastest production car at the 1957 Daytona Speed Week, posting a 134.128 mph flying mile. Curiously, the top speed was short of 1956 300

*When you slid behind the wheel ▶ of the Chrysler 300C you knew you were driving an awesome machine.*

*The famous Chrysler ▶ 392-cid Hemi engine could haze the tires at will. Period reviews clocked 0 to 60 times in the 8.4-second range.*

standards (that car had notched a best of 139.37 mph) but Chrysler's unofficial mark of 145.7 mph at the Chelsea Proving Grounds suggested that this was in fact the strongest "Letter Car" to date.

Chrysler's newest engineering advance in 1957 was torsion bar suspension, and all Mopar cars thus vaulted ahead of the pack in their cornering potential—none more so than the 300C. Inches lower than its line mates, with beefier brakes and that revamped suspension, the 300 was a crisp-handling car. Firm riding, too—roughly 40 percent stiffer than the neighboring New Yorker series – meant the "Letter Cars" rode harder, if not harsh.

1957 marked the first year that Chrysler's fleet flagship could be had in a convertible form. Elite ($5,359) and exclusive (484 built) these cars were at the top of the class of 1957. Few cars before or since have so artfully captured the combination of blistering performance and sleek styling.

*◄ Stylist Virgil Exner's handiwork included a sleek set of tailfins— among the decade's best.*

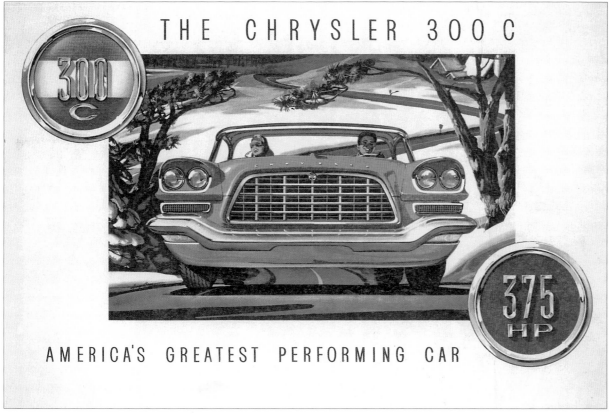

*◄ Nothing more needed to be suggested in Chrysler advertising than the 300C logo and 375-hp.*

# DeSoto Fireflite

*◄ This was the indisputable high water mark—never before or again would people spend as much time looking at the back of a new car design as they did the front.*

ARE THESE THE FINEST FINS of the Fifties? True connoisseurs of the fender wing know this styling feature as a creature of the Fifties (though the first fins date from 1948). But, the golden era of the tailfin began in 1957 and stretched through the end of the decade. This was the indisputable high water mark—never before or again would people spend as much time looking at the back of a new car design as they did the front. The tall, tapered fender lines of the '57 Chevy have long been admired by auto buffs and the '59 Cadillac's "Rocket Tail" became (as we shall see) perhaps the ultimate auto icon of the decade.

That said, there may have been no finer a fin formed in the Fifties than those found on the '57 DeSoto Fireflite. 1957 was the ultimate expression of Chrysler Designer Virgil Exner's Forward Look. While every Mopar sported a variation of this style, none captured it more cleanly than DeSoto. It was a long, low, sweeping shape, with a dart-like profile. A wide and handsome chrome lattice grille flanked a long, oval bumper up front. Complementing the look was a set of flowing, shark-like fenders in back, capped by elegant, "Tri-Tower" taillights.

Fireflite was the mainstream mainstay of the DeSoto lineup. It was the third of four series available in 1957, slotted below the high

*◄ Sweeping tailfins were the styling signature of the Virgil Exner "Forward Look" cars of 1957 and was especially well-executed in the De Sotos*

*Tailfins were a statement promoted by Chrysler in the late 1950s and no one said it better than De Soto Fireflite Sportsman.*

*Smooth shifting and stoutly built, the TorqueFlite automatic transmission earned rave reviews in its supporting role to Chrysler V-8s.*

performance Adventurers and above the Firesweep and Firedome lines. Powered by a 341-cid, 295-hp hemi-head V-8, rolling on a 126-inch wheelbase, six models were built, including 1,151 Fireflite convertibles, and 7,217 Sportsman hardtop coupes. In a year when the average American family earned $5,000, a convertible and hardtop like the ones featured here stickered for $3,890 and $3,614, respectively.

Overall, DeSoto sold 117,000 cars in 1957, good enough for 11th place, industry-wide. Looking at the fine lines of these Fireflites, it's hard to believe that DeSoto was on the endangered list, but it was. 1957 turned out to be DeSoto's last best year. Caught in the crunch between Chrysler and Dodge, DeSoto became the odd brand out, departing after the 1961 model year.

▲ Quad headlights were not legal in all 48 states during the 1957 production run so many De Sotos still exist in both two- and four-lamp versions.

◄ The muscle under the Fireflite Sportsman's hood was a version of the famed Hemi engine.

◄ Brand identity was something De Soto hoped to stamp on the automotive world of 1957.

# Dodge D-100 Sweptside

◀ *Among the changes for the 1958 Sweptside was a revamped two-tone paint scheme.*

DODGE HAD A PROBLEM. They were a day late and a dollar short. Late, because Chevy was already out of the gate with the dressy, upscale Cameo Carrier pickup (and Ford was soon to follow, with their half car/half truck Ranchero). Short, because there wasn't enough money on hand for anything more than a modest makeover. At the time, Dodge's share of the pickup truck market was a slim 7 percent – not exactly a profit center.

If cash was lacking, creativity was not. Dodge's Joe Berr found inspiration in a station wagon. A two door Dodge Suburban, specifically, which supplied a set of long, sweeping tailfins that were fitted to a ½ ton truck with Custom Cab. Mind you, these weren't just any fins. As we've seen, '57 Chrysler products were sporting some of the Fifties flashiest fenders, thanks to Virgil Exner's "Forward Look." The tall, graceful fins looked particularly dashing when grafted onto the long wheelbase pickup. Berr, Manager of Dodge's Special Equipment Group, orchestrated the facelift (which was really more of a tail lift, given the prominence of the fins.) Special chrome trim pieces were added to accent the striking side view, while up front, all 1957 Dodges had hooded, "frenched" headlights. The Suburban's rear bumper was pressed into service out back, as was the tailgate, though it had to be trimmed to fit.

STRAIGHT OUT OF TOMORROW ➤

GILSDORF MOTOR CO.
19 E. FIRST ST.
FOND DU LAC WIS.

## The Sweptside 100

Now you can add _new_ prestige
to your business with the Dodge
Sweptside 100. Here's the most
exciting new pick-up on the road...
and it offers the most V-8 power and
the most payload capacity of the
low-priced three. See it! Drive it soon!

_exciting new_ **Dodge** pick-up

The finished product was wrapped in a two-tone coat of paint and wide whitewalls were fitted at the corners.

Owing to fiscal constraints, Sweptside's magic was limited to show and not go. Beneath the new sheet metal, it was business as usual for this Dodge. Buyers could choose from either a 230-cid, 120-hp straight six or an optional, 315-cid, 204-hp V-8. Gear changing was handled by either a three-speed manual or available push-button LoadFlite automatic transmission.

More "clothes horse" than workhorse, Sweptside, Cameo and Ranchero presaged pickups of half a century hence. While we think nothing of using trucks as grocery getters and city cruisers today, 50 years ago, high-style trucks with car-like comfort were largely unheard of. Sweptside production continued in limited numbers through early 1959, when it was superseded by the Sweptline series.

_Dodge changed pickup truck ▲_
_styling with the 1957 Sweptside._

_The most striking feature of ▶_
_the Sweptside Dodge pickups_
_was the long, lean finned_
_fenders—borrowed from the_
_Dodge Suburban two-door_
_station wagon._

◀ Inside the Sweptside models in each year was the normal business-like pickup look with nothing as fancy as the exterior.

▲ The Forward Look logo looked especially good on the Dodge Sweptside pickups.

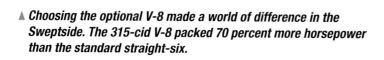

▲ Choosing the optional V-8 made a world of difference in the Sweptside. The 315-cid V-8 packed 70 percent more horsepower than the standard straight-six.

# 1957 Dual-Ghia

◄ Long, low and sleek, the Dual-Ghia was exotic in its day and scarce then as now.

**M**OST TIMES, show cars are just that: cars made for shows that rarely go into production. The exceptions have oft times been exceptional – the kind of cars that people dream about. But, sometimes the dream doesn't last, fading like puddles on a hot summer day. Count the Dual-Ghia among these fantasy casualties.

Renowned Stylist Virgil Exner penned many memorable designs in the 1950s, including the Dodge Firearrow concept cars that made the show circuit in 1953 and '54. Chrysler had no plans to put Firearrow

into production, but a well-to-do industrialist named Eugene Casaroll thought otherwise. Smitten with the styling, Casaroll bought the rights from Chrysler to build it, and engaged Engineer Paul Farago to help transform Firearrow from show car to "street car of desire."

Dual-Ghia combined European coach building (via Ghia) with American mechanicals (courtesy of Chrysler). Ghia modified the frame of a '56 Dodge and fitted it with a sleek body of hand- formed steel. The rolling chassis were then shipped back to

◄ It may have seemed like a 1950s dream but the Dual-Ghia instrument panel was the real thing in 1957.

*Along the way from show car to showroom, Dual-Ghia picked up a set of tasteful tail fins.*

*Below:* **In 1957, Mallory Electric showed off the exotic Dual Ghia with its ignition parts.**

Dual Motors in Detroit, for installation of the drive train and final assembly.

The finest materials were used – brass instead of lesser metals, Connolly hides for the seats, a trunk covered with felt and a hood lined with quilted leather. A 315-cid Dodge Hemi V-8 provided the thrust and was offered with horsepower ranging from 230 to 285. Top performing models could sprint from 0 to 60 in 8.6 seconds, and the low-slung form clung to corners.

Dual-Ghias were improbably priced and impossible to get. Having the requisite $7,741 cash wasn't enough, unless you also had connections. The owner catered to the rich and famous (Dual-Ghia clientele included Frank Sinatra and Sammy Davis Jr.) Casaroll was burned on his pricing, though, losing an estimated $4,000 per car on the labor-intensive Dual-Ghias since each car took an estimated 1,500 hours to build. That, and Chrysler's planned change to a different platform signaled the end of the line. Though the first Dual-Ghias were followed by a second generation 1960 L6.4 coupe, it was the last gasp for these elegant, multi-culturals. Casaroll quit the car business after just 117 Dual-Ghias had been built.

▲ *The stylish Italian-American Dual-Ghia attracted attention on North American highways in 1957.*

◄ *Beneath the quilted leather hood liner and fiberglass insulation was a Hemi V-8 —available in 230-hp four-barrel version or a two-fours setup that netted 285 hp.*

◄ *Few 1950s cars still draw more double-takes than the unique 1950s El Morocco—like this 1957 El Morocco convertible.*

WHAT DO YOU GET when you cross a Chevy and a Cadillac? The answer, in one man's eyes, was the El Morocco. In the mid-Fifties, a Detroit businessman and car buff named Ruben Allender hit upon the idea of combining a Chevy Bel Air with some Cadillac styling cues. The result he dubbed the El Morocco – a not so subtle attempt to ride on the classy coattails of Cadillac's Eldorado.

El Moroccos were produced for two years – 1956 and '57 – with conversions done in Allender's Detroit warehouse. No mechanical modifications were made, though cosmetic changes to the body were substantial. On 1957 models, the front end featured prominent, "Dagmar" bumper guards

framing a wide, grate-like grille. In back, the Chevy's classic tailfins were shorn and overlaid with "Cadillesque" fins, while below was a beefy bumper with embedded lights. The profile view revealed bright work on the rear quarter panels, echoing the exclusive look of the Cadillac Eldorado Brougham. Ditto the special hubcaps, which were remarkably reminiscent of Cadillac's Saber Spoke wheel covers. El Morocco badging was added to the hood, deck lid and the steering wheel center. Interiors were largely standard issue Chevy.

*Motor Trend* wrote about Allender in September, 1956. The magazine got caught up in the owner's optimism for the El Morocco's prospects, gushing, "We can't help but agree that a Chevrolet-based

The 1957 El Morocco wheel ▶
covers had a very intentional
resemblance to the 1957
Cadillac's "saber spokes."

A large part of the El Morocco' ▼
unique look was in back where
Cadillac-style tailfins replaced
the Chevrolet fins and a
different bumper.

miniature (Cadillac) at $3,250 complete should be a hot seller."

Or not.

By 1957, the price of an El Morocco convertible had been reduced to $2,950. Even so, that was still about $500 more than a comparable Bel Air, and clearly, the cars were more Chevy than Caddy. Moreover, Allender's production and distribution capabilities were extremely limited. Though he sought to sell his wares through Chevy dealers, GM didn't see the percentage in this. Even *Motor Trend* allowed as much back in 1956: "It is not logical for Chevrolet outlets to handle the El Morocco."

The combined weight of these facts forced the car to sink after only its second season. Total production for both years is thought to have been no more than three-dozen cars, of which 16 are estimated to have been 1957 models.

▲ The El Morocco's interior was heavily Chevy Bel Air with some minor changes.

◀ The 1957 El Morocco power plant was pure Chevrolet V-8.

◀ A 1956 El Morocco shared the cover of the September Motor Trend with a Facel-Vega.

◄ *In 1958, the Ranchero received dual headlights with its new front-end clip.*

F OR EVERY one pickup that works for a living today, another three will never see anything in their boxes more exotic than a sack of grass seed. It was a lot more black and white in the '50s – cars were cars and trucks were trucks – until car-truck hybrids like the Ford Ranchero started changing the rules.

Ranchero wasn't the first to plow this ground in the U.S. market. Studebaker's Coupe-Express and Hudson's sedan pickups pioneered here decades earlier. By the time that the first Ranchero rolled onto the roadways in 1957, we'd already seen trucks like Chevy's Cameo push the envelope for creature comforts in the previously Spartan world

of pickups. But, Ranchero took it a step further. If Cameo was a truck with some car leanings, Ranchero was a car first, with truck portions added. It was a station wagon, specifically; the two door Ranch Wagon, with a pickup box instead of a back seat/cargo area. Standard and Custom models were offered, and engine options ranged from a 223-cid, 144-hp inline six, to a 292-cid, 212-hp V8. Three-speed manual was standard, with overdrive or Ford-O-Matic optional. Because Ranchero was essentially a Ranch Wagon, options like a power seat or power windows – at the time, exotic in cars and unheard of in pickups – could be added.

Period ads for Ford's "half and half" ½-ton played up the new model's split personality. Ranchero's

◄ *The cargo area of the 1957 and '58 Ranchero was taken from Ford's spacious 1957 station wagons.*

*Ranchero's comfortable cabin was far more car than truck.* ▶

*Only Ranchero held over Ford's round light look from 1957 to 1958.* ▼

"truckish" cargo capacity and six-foot load floor shared ink with the available power amenities. "Ranchero combines sleeves-up spunk with coats-on style."

The concept caught people's fancy, and with its "modest" base price of $1,920, Ranchero sold swiftly - 21,705 in '57. When it returned in 1958 for its second season, styling made an interesting departure from the rest of the lineup. The front end featured a fine-mesh grille and dual quad headlights. A fake hood scoop rounded out the T-Bird inspired facelift, which curiously enough, wasn't accompanied by a tail lift. Ranchero kept the canted fins and big, round lights that it wore in 1957, while the rest of Ford's cars went to split, oval lights. The engine choices expanded to include a 352-cid, 300-hp V-8.

Power was up, but sales were down, skidding to 9,950 units. But every automaker was taking on water in 1958. Ford knew that the idea had legs and hung onto it. The move paid off. Ranchero continued as a productive part of the lineup through 1979.

▲ Canadian buyers could choose a Ranchero at Ford dealers or select one at the local Meteor and Monarch dealers.

► Ford made a big splash in its advertising for the all-new 1957 Ranchero.

◄ Unless you looked at the back end, you would have thought this was another good looking 1958 Ford car.

# Hudson Hornet Hollywood

*◄ This was the final curtain call for the Hudson and it was not renewed after the 1957 model year.*

THE FIFTIES claimed the lives of several auto marques, and left others on the critical list. Among the casualties, Nash and Hudson, which had their swan song year in 1957. American Motors President George Romney axed the big cars from the lineup at midyear, concentrating company resources on the compact, economy-minded Ramblers.

So if you gotta go, might as well have a Hollywood ending, like our featured, 1957 Hornet Custom Hollywood – one of 438 built. For '57, Hudson was strictly Hornets: Super and Custom series cars, available as either a four-door sedan or two-door

Hollywood hardtop. A Custom series coupe like this one had a sticker price of $3,101.

This was the second (and as it turned out, final) year of Hudson's V-Line styling. The most notable features of these designs were an enormous, v-shaped, egg-crate grille and body sides busy with creases and chrome trim strips. Color charts expanded to include five tri-tone schemes for Custom models. Rear fenders sprouted small tailfins, must-have styling, in what was the ultimate year for fins. Fins were so popular in fact that the Hornet had *four.* The new rear appendages were matched by twin fin trim on both front fenders, too. The fin count was up, but the cars were down. A flatter roof design, a switch from 15- to 14-inch

*◄ Mini-fin treatment in the nose area of the 1957 Hudson Hornet Hollywood was very unusual.*

*Talk about reclining seats!* ▶
*Hudson's front bench folded flat*
*for bedroom-like comfort—albeit*
*a bedroom with a steering wheel.*

HUDSON FOR 1957

POWER'S UP

PRICE'S DOWN

JIM MOLON
867 New Yo
Altadena, Cali

wheels and lower profile tires knocked about two inches off the Hornet's height.

Under the hood was a big power boost. AMC's 250-cid V-8 was bored out to 327 cubic inches. With four-barrel carburetion and dual exhaust, horsepower was a healthy 255 (up from 190.) Inside, Hornets had front seats that folded flat back to form a bed – a feature that made the cars popular with teenage drive-in patrons and unpopular with their parents. The fine specimen seen here is as loaded as a "bee" could be for 1957. No doubt inspired by the name (Flashaway Hydra-Matic), the buyer sprang for the automatic transmission ($232), power steering ($100) and the ultra rare, Weather Eye air conditioning, which had a price tag of $415.

American Motors lost a sobering $11,833,200 in '57 – this, despite a gain of almost 10 percent in product output. AMC soldiered on, but Hudson's days were numbered. Rambler rode 1958's recession to record sales. By then, Hudson (along with Nash) were history.

▲ Tri-tone paint and chrome-laden, V-line styling gave the '57 Hudson enough flash for any Hollywood opening.

◄ The taillights were *de riguer* **styling staples for 1957 cars including the Hornet Hollywood.**

◄ *Met bodies were supplied by the Fisher and Ludlow company of Birmingham, England.*

THE METROPOLITAN was a multinational mini-car, an early pioneer in the subcompact segment.  Sold from 1954 to 1962, they were badged variously as Nash, Hudson or Metropolitan. No matter the nameplate, the cars were virtually the same, save grilles or emblem differences. Though aimed at the U.S. market, the cars were built in Great Britain.

The bodies were provided by Fisher & Ludlow of Birmingham, England. Production Mets traced their design roots to the pen of stylist Bill Flajole. A prototype dubbed the NXI (for Nash Experimental International) was first shown in 1950, making the rounds to gauge public acceptance.

The Met's driveline paired the veteran Austin A40 four-cylinder motor with a three-speed manual transmission.  The four-banger displaced 73 cubic inches, and it was rated at a mere 42 hp.  However, that was more than enough to propel the 1,800 lb. flyweight down the road to a top speed of 70 mph.  Of course, Metropolitan buyers were more interested in thrift than thrust, and the first generation cars proved truly frugal, returning as much as 40 miles per gallon.

The Metropolitan was effectively a two-seater. The utility back seat was essentially a padded package tray, more suitable to small parcels than small people. Six cubic feet of storage space was available in the trunk (about the same size as a modern day Mazda Miata), though getting *to* the storage was the

◄ *While they were sold by both Nash and Hudson dealers in 1957, they were simply badged as Metropolitans.*

The Metropolitans were basically ▲ two-seat cars with a little room for more.

A continental kit along with ▲ two-tone paint schemes added a distinctly American feeling to the British-built Metropolitan.

The Metropolitan just about ▼ cornered the market on "cute" in the 1950s.

trick. Mets didn't have a trunk lid for outside access until 1959.

A second generation Metropolitan appeared in mid-1956. These series 1500 cars included both show and go changes. Gone was the faux hood scope and added was an egg-crate grille with "M" badging. Side on, a zigzag molding traced a front to rear path, and served as the borderline for two-tone paint jobs. On the go side, an A50 Austin motor replaced the former A40.

Displacement rose to 91 cid, horsepower to 52, and top speed was now 80 mph. Prices were set at $1,527 for a coupe, $1,551 for a convertible.

The car that defined "cute" *for* the 1950s was ultimately a product *of* the '50s. Production stopped in 1960, though leftovers continued to sell for another two years. In all, over 90,000 Metropolitans were sold in the U.S., and pioneering econo-cars like this pretty '57 continue to be crowd pleasers at car shows today.

# The Metropolitan *"1500"*

**MEET THE WORLD'S SMARTEST SMALLER CAR!** The Metropolitan "1500" provides smart, sound, sensible transportation for two people plus, in either of two distinctive body styles—Hardtop Coupe and dashing Convertible. You'll like the sparkling, yet thrifty power . . . the sensational handling ease in traffic . . . the responsiveness on the open road. Here, truly, is luxury in miniature . . . "A watch-charm Rolls-Royce" as Devon Francis described the Metropolitan in Popular Science Monthly.

METROPOLITAN "1500" CONVERTIBLE

▲ *A perky 1500 convertible graces the cover of this 1957 Metropolitan brochure.*

◄ *The pint-size power plant was enlarged to a robust 52 horsepower in 1956. The Austin A-50 engine offered Met drivers more than 40 mpg.*

# Studebaker Golden Hawk

◄ *Studebaker's in-house hot rod in this Golden Age of Horsepower was the Golden Hawk.*

THE HIGH PERFORMANCE spark touched off in 1955 by Chevy's V-8 powered "Hot Ones" was in full flame by 1957. Studebaker's in-house hot rod in this Golden Age of Horsepower was the Golden Hawk.

Studebaker coupes provided one of the most interesting styling subtexts of the Fifties. The elegant, Euro-look "Loewy Coupes" of 1953 and '54 evolved into the outrageous 1955 Speedster, then settled into a final, extended evolution as the Hawk series of 1956 to '64. The hottest of the Hawks for 1957—the Golden—wore a mild facelift from 1956 versions. It was a tail-lift, to be precise.

The nascent tailfins of 1956 were now fully grown, canting slightly outward. Two-toning was reigned in from '56 levels, now restricted to tailfin inserts. Inside, the double hues were carried over in the vinyl interior, and an engine-turned dash gave the sport coupe an appropriately sporty appearance. Studebaker dabbled with an upscale variation, too. Dubbed the Golden Hawk 400, it boasted pleated leather upholstery, flared armrests, a carpeted trunk, and probably sold fewer copies than its numerical namesake.

The '56 Golden Hawk packed 275 hp, thanks to its 352-cid V-8. However, it also packed on a lot of unwanted pounds, thanks to the cast iron

◄ *Far Left: The 1957 Golden Hawk showed a South Bend-car could literally keep up with the best of the Big Three, if only on the highway.*

*Two-toning and an engine-* ▶
*turned dash added a shot*
*of sportiness to the 1957*
*Golden Hawk's cabin.*

*Even with strong advertising,* ▼
*just 4,356 Golden Hawks were*
*sold in the 1957 model year.*

Command performance for safety—the Studebaker Golden Hawk puts you in command with a built-in supercharger for extra power the instant you need it...puts you in command with Twin Traction for driving power in both rear wheels...and puts you in command with the most effective brakes. Put yourself in command of a Golden Hawk at your dealer's, today!

**Studebaker-Packard**
CORPORATION

*Where pride of Workmanship comes first!*

girth of the Packard motor. The drive train alone weighed some 900 lbs., and accordingly, almost 60 percent of the car's weight rested on the front axle. Critics pounded South Bend for the car's "nose-heavy" nature, resulting understeer, and light-tailed launch difficulties. When the Golden Hawk returned in 1957, it was about 100 lbs. lighter – all removed from the front end. Studebaker substituted its 289 V-8—a husky motor in its own right, but positively svelte compared to the Packard mill. Horsepower was identical to 1956 levels – 275 – thanks to the addition of a McCullouch, belt-driven supercharger. Slimmed down, with better balance, an improved front suspension and a new, limited slip differential, this Hawk could fly , and the critics sang its praises.

The year-end tally showed that Studebaker had sold 4,356 of their $3,182 Golden Hawks. The car played a key role in the lineup. It gave the independent automaker a car that was hot enough to keep up with the Big Three's best, and cool enough to chase traffic into Studebaker showrooms.

*While some chose vertical tailfins, Studebaker canted their fins in order to blend in with a body style designed several years before.*

*The lighter 289-cid Studebaker motor used in the 1957 outperformed the heavier Packard V-8 used in 1956. Better balance and performance ensued and "auto wags" wagged faster.*

# Buick Century Caballero

◄ *All the glitz didn't play well in the gloomy 1958 economic climate and Buick sales sagged with other automakers.*

It's a re-chromer's dream. Safe to say, making the shiny parts of a 1958 Buick shiny again has helped put more than one car restorer's kids through college. Beneath all this chrome is the Century Caballero – a hardtop, '58 Buick station wagon. Hardtops were the rage in the 1950s. The pillarless profile when you rolled down the windows lent an open air feel akin to a convertible, but without the cost or compromises that came with a ragtop. It was inevitable that the hardtop craze would extend to station wagons. In the days before minivans and SUVs, wagons were the vehicles of choice for families. Few are the Baby Boomers whose childhood memories don't include road trips seen through the back seat window of a wagon.

Actually, Caballero was one of two hardtop station wagons built by Buick in 1957 and '58. One was based on the Special series, and Caballero was derived from the up-level Century line. Buick designs for 1958 were pretty outrageous. Up front, a gaping grille with a noble name. The "Fashion-Aire Dynastar Grille" was packed full of small, chrome cubes (160 to be exact, thereby furnishing the answer to a future Buick trivia question). The profile view showed four ventiports flanking the fender tops. Below, a shiny sweep spear arched

*Its "twin-tower" taillights ▶*
*were part of the Caballero's*
*prodigious rear image in 1958.*

*The Buick Caballero originally ▼*
*appeared as a choice 1957 model.*

downward, giving way to a bullet-shaped, brushed aluminum panel. In back, a massive bumper was bookended by Twin-Tower taillights. Overall, chrome was applied, as GM Design Chief Bill Mitchell later observed, "with a trowel."

Buick described their 1958 models as, "Big Bold and Buoyant." But, the U.S. economy in 1958 was anything but, suffering through its worst recession since the Second World War. As Buick was to find out, it's hard to sell flash when your buyers are short of cash. Auto sales slumped industry-wide and on the leaden wings of heavy-handed styling, Buick slid from fourth to fifth among carmakers.

Mid-price cars like Caballero were particularly hard hit. Where 10,186 had sold for 1957, the number sank to 4,456 in '58.

◄ The open hardtop styling of the Caballero gives a good look at the Buick's colorful cabin.

◄ The grinning Dynastar grille put a memorable face on the "Air Born B-58" Buick Century Caballero.

# 1957-'58
# *Chevy Cameo Carrier*

◄ *Cameo combined car-like style and comfort elements with the traditionally Spartan form of the pickup.*

IN THE 1990'S, Chrysler made much about the "Cab Forward" design of their big sedans. Much ado, but hardly new. True cab forward styling dates back at least forty years earlier, to a classy pickup truck called the Chevy Cameo Carrier. When it first appeared in 1955, it promptly turned the light truck world on its ear. Cameo combined car-like style and comfort elements with the traditionally Spartan form of the pickup. 1955 was a watershed year for Chevy's passenger cars, so borrowing design cues for the Cameo seemed like a natural. Between the hooded headlights sat a big, chrome, egg-crate grille, lifted right from the new car line.

The cab was *literally* forward: A- and B-pillars canted towards the truck's nose, with wraparound glass in front and (optionally) in back. The fiberglass rear fenders formed a smooth, clean line from front to back. Inside, the two-tone interior was set off by a custom stitched pattern and a face-to-face view of the new, wedge-shaped instrument panel. All Chevy's 1955 pickups rolled on a shorter wheelbase with a wider track, and the new V-8 motors that were the power behind Chevy's passenger cars were also available on Cameo.

◄ *The Cameo Carrier styling first appeared in the 1955 Chevy truck lineup. This 1958 edition is the rarest version.*

The basic formula was repeated, with minor variations, for the next two years. In 1958, the game changed again, and this shift signaled Cameo's demise. 1958 was a restyle year for Chevy's light trucks and many of Cameo's signature style elements were incorporated into the whole Fleetside lineup. The result was a light truck line that looked more special, and a special model that was suddenly less so. In addition, the semi-custom truck idea that Cameo had championed since 1955 spawned competitive models from other automakers. Dodge had joined the fray with their Sweptside trucks in '57, and that same year, Ford went a step further, with the sedan pickup Rancheros.

All of the above plus the dreary 1958 economy conspired to seal Cameo's fate—a victim of its own success. But, even as Chevy was preparing to retire it, they were at work on a replacement. The car-truck synergy was channeled in a different direction, to the El Camino—a Ranchero fighter that would roll out in 1959.

*The Chevrolet Cameo Carrier ▲ interior was upscale for a 1957 pickup.*

*Chevrolet posed the Cameo ◄ Carrier in front of a mansion in its 1957 pickup brochure.*

▲ Contrast the 1958 styling with this fine
1957, the last of the first generation
Cameo Carriers.

◄ The 1957 Chevrolet Cameo Carrier
was powered by a 265-cid, 155-hp
Trademaster V-8.

# Chevy Impala

*Popular with the public and the automotive press, the 1955 through '57 models cemented Chevy's position in the hearts and sales charts of America's car buyers.*

T ALK ABOUT a tough act to follow! The 1958 Chevy lineup arrived on the heels of a three-year cycle of cars that were destined to become Fifties classics. Popular with the public and the automotive press, the 1955 through '57 models cemented Chevy's position in the hearts and sales charts of America's car buyers.

Against that backdrop, the 1958 models arrived. The first clean-sheet new Chevys in three years were playing catch-up. While these were GM's first wave of longer-lower-wider cars, the other members of the Big Three had been selling this look since '57, and the auto industry as a whole

would ride it right into the Sixties. Slotted in at the top of Chevy's Bel Air series was a new model called Impala. Impala's first time, flagship run proved so successful that the name became a permanent part of the lineup lexicon for decades to follow.

In a year famous for busy designs at GM, the 1958 Impala's style was less glitzy than most, and particularly successful from the back, where the gull-wing fenders arched gracefully over triple taillights. Inside, Impala had plenty of flash. Hop into the color-coordinated, striped seats and you wrapped your hands around a sporty, boomerang-spoked steering wheel. Beneath the skin, Impala

*The new-for-1958 Chevrolet Impala logo showed the African antelope leaping between a pair of checkered flags.*

The Chevrolet Impala cabin was ▶ highlighted by a sporty two-spoke steering wheel, aluminum trim on the dash and door panels plus color-keyed upholstery.

The 1958 Chevrolet Impala two-▼ door hardtop is the focus of this ad from that year.

The Impala Sport Coupe—every window of every Chevrolet is Safety Plate Glass.

**EXCITEMENT RIDES WITH YOU** *every mile you roll in your* new **CHEVROLET.** *At rest or on the road, this sleek style-setter promises action, gaiety, glamor—and it keeps its promises beautifully. Come aboard and take the key to the happiest traveling on the highway!*

One look at those saucy lines and you know this new Chevy's ready to shove off for wherever you say.

Just name your course—a bustling highway, a tumbling mountain road or a side street to the corner grocery. Here's the car with the kind of eager-going gait that turns any route into a pleasure cruise.

You'll see what we mean the first time you feel the quick-sprinting torque of Chevrolet's new Turbo-Thrust V8* whisk you up a steep hill. Or learn how this engine loves to shrink the miles out where they're long and lonesome.

And you'll find still more to be proud of in the way Chevy takes the wrinkles out of aging roads. There's a choice of two completely new rides—Full Coil suspension as standard and a real air ride* besides. Each is engineered to achieve a gentleness you'd expect only in the costliest cars.

The plain truth is that you're missing one of the most rewarding experiences on the road if you haven't yet taken the wheel of this new Chevrolet. It's an over-sight your dealer will gladly remedy....
Chevrolet Division of General Motors, Detroit 2, Michigan.   *Optional at extra cost

CHEVROLET

may have packed on some pounds, but it was quality weight. The longer (117.5-inch) wheelbase, stiffer X-member chassis and smoother coil spring rear suspension made for a comfortable highway car. *Car Life's* Jim Whipple found, "...little or no discernable body shake or vibration even on the roughest surfaces."

A thrifty 145-hp six-cylinder engine was standard fare, but if you were in the market for something hotter, Chevy would be happy to accommodate you. A trio of optional 283-cid V-8's ranged from 185-250 hp. Newly available was the 348-cid Turbo-Thrust V-8, offered in versions rated at 250 to 315 hp. After a shakedown at GM's Proving Grounds, *Car Life* gave the 348 the thumbs up, noting that it would cruise comfortably at 100 mph.

The 1958 Impala has always been something of a sleeper amongst fifties classics. While it's never drawn as wide a following among collectors as the '55 through '57 Chevys, Impala was a smash hit when new. Even in recession-wracked 1958, the top-line Chevy rolled up over 181,000 sales.

▲ The gull wing rear treatment was standard on all 1958 Chevys but the triple taillights and faux roof-mounted air scoop were Impala exclusives.

◄ Buyers of 1958 Impalas could choose a variety of V-8s including small blocks with up to 250 fuel-injected horsepower and the big block 348-cid V-8 with as much as 315 hp.

◄ *Ford put a lot of money into researching buyer trends but their fickle choices shifted between the time the car was designed and when it was introduced.*

WHAT FORD DIDN'T KNOW—couldn't know—when the Edsel was being planned in the mid-Fifties was this. By the time that the car arrived, the customers that they intended to woo would all be sitting firmly on their wallets, riding out a stormy U.S. recession. As a result, the Edsel opened the door to 1958, rolled outside and promptly drove off a cliff.

It could have been worse. During product development, Ford was contemplating what to call their new model. They went so far as to hire a poetess to render a list of potential names. The resulting register included such gems as "Utopian Turtle top" and "Mongoose Civique" (really rolls off the tongue, doesn't it?) Fortunately, Ford had the good sense to pass on those, settling at last on Edsel – the name of Henry Ford's son (and curiously, a choice strongly opposed by Edsel's son, Henry Ford II).

Edsel was distinctively styled and gadget-laden. Coming or going, there was little doubt of what you were looking at. Squinting cat-eye taillights greeted those behind, and the front view was dominated by an oversize, horse-collar grille, set between dual quad headlights. The side view and overall dimensions were more conventional: a rounded rectangle with some interesting rises in front and rear fender lines.

◄ *The Edsel "horse collar" grille is long on character. You could always spot the 1958 Edsel from six blocks away.*

Edsel's engine choices included ▶ the 361-cid, 303-hp V-8 in the Ranger and Pacer or the 410-cid, 345-hp power plant in the Corsair and Citation.

Edsels equipped with "Tele-Touch Drive" automatics ▲ had gear choices in a steering wheel hub pod. Driving speed was read in a revolving-drum speedometer.

The cabin was vintage, Flash Gordon Fifties fare. Push-button controls for transmission were in fashion, here curiously centered in the steering wheel hub. The speedometer dispensed with the traditional, horizontal thermometer-style strip, in favor of a rounded, revolving drum. Ford's rollout for Edsel was nothing if not ambitious. Seventeen models were offered, spread among the Ranger, Pacer, Corsair and Citation series.

Edsel didn't sell badly so much as it sold badly below Ford's inflated expectations (triple digit sales were anticipated). Styling of succeeding year's models was progressively more subdued, but it didn't matter. The "disconnect" between predicted sales and market reality had dealt Edsel a fatal blow. A lack of differentiation with the established mid-size Mercury line limited sales, and a quick reputation for uneven build quality didn't help, either. The combined effect branded the cars as failures. And that's a shame. Both the car and the man named Edsel deserved a better assessment.

Fact is, Edsel was better than its reputation. The wild styling, so panned by critics almost 50 years ago, is now cherished by collectors. Ultimately, the worst thing that Edsel could be accused of was terminally bad timing.

▲ *The flat deck of the Edsel is complemented nicely by its cat's-eye taillights.*

# Packard Hawk

◄ *Attempts to streamline the 1958 Packard Hawk brought unfavorable comparisons with a vacuum cleaner in the view of some observers.*

PACKARD WAS on life support. The once-proud rival to Cadillac as America's luxury leader had, by 1958, fallen on the hardest of times. The patient's health proxy was cash-strapped Studebaker, and the prognosis was plain and simple: keep the Packard brand alive and hope for a miracle cure. Practically speaking, this meant fielding four re-badged Studebakers for '58, and biding time until enough funds were found to finance a true rebirth of the grand marque.

The most intriguing of the quartet was the Packard Hawk. "Intriguing," though, would probably *not* be

the first word used to describe the Packard Hawk by most car shoppers in 1958 – peculiar might be a more popular choice. Starting with the Studebaker Hawk body, Packard stylists added gold Mylar inserts on the tailfins, and vinyl armrests that wrapped over the windowsills (an idea borrowed from vintage airplane cockpits). The deck lid gained a vestigial spare tire bulge. As when found on Chrysler products of the period, this dubious design device was eventually and inevitably referred to as a toilet seat. Up front was a great, gaping, fish-mouth of a grille, backed up by a large faux air scoop on the fiber glass hood. Taken together, the car was—to use the current vernacular—*so not*

◄ *The black paint accentuates the positives of this once proud marque. Packard would pass into history following the 1958 model year.*

*Packard.* And so, not surprisingly, it didn't sell, registering 588 takers for the $4,000 asking price.

Whatever one made of the looks, there was no disputing the car's performance. Wielding the supercharged Studebaker 289 V-8, linked to a three-speed Flight-O-Matic automatic transmission, the "Packardbaker" could turn 0-60 in about nine seconds, and hit a terminal speed of 125 mph. Revamped shocks and springs made it a good road handler, too.

Inside, the P-Hawk offered fleeting glimpses of Packard's luxury heritage, most notably in its tan, pleated premium leather interior, with padded dash and door tops. An engine-turned casing held a full complement of Stewart Warner gauges, lending a sporty look to the big coupe's cabin.

The Hawk made an odd finale to the symphony that had once been Packard. Like rock n' roll at a royal reception, it seemed curiously out of character.

Studebaker lineage was hard to miss from any angle. It was one reason why Packard purists shunned the hybrid Hawks.

The McCullouch supercharger kicked in past 3,000 rpms offering 275 horses in the Studebaker mill. The Packard Hawk could suck the doors off of many contemporary cars.

# Cadillac Series 62

*◄ The nobly-proportioned 1959 Cadillacs stretched 225 inches or more than 18 feet! It was more than a match for many garages.*

THE '59 CADILLAC STORY begins at the end. At the tail end, specifically, where a pair of the decade's most audacious tailfins resided. Though linked indelibly to the Fifties, high-flying fins were in reality a product of the 1940s, and were said to have been inspired by a WWII fighter plane. (It was the Lockheed P-38 Lightning.) The first set of tailfins sprouted from the fenders of the 1948 Cadillac. Largely dormant through much of the following decade, fins were not *truly* in until post-1955 America. They reached their peak – literally – in the period from 1957 through 1959.

The poster boy for these peaked pinions was this car. The '59 Cadillac's "Rocket Tail" was a thing to

behold. Taking off just aft of the back seats, the rear fenders swept up and back to a summit 42 inches above ground. Truly towering they were, and each adorned with a pair of egg-shaped taillights. Just below, massive chrome afterburner-style housings held the backup lights. By 1959, Americans had seen fins of all flavors, but no one had seen anything quite like this before.

Above the bumper was a small rear grille, intended to echo a front grille that was anything *but* small. It featured a great, grinning mouth full of mesh, with double dual headlights above and recessed parking and turn signals below. Collectively, it was, as one magazine put it, "...a massive frontal treatment."

*◄ Cadillac's tailfins measured nearly 3-½ feet from pavement to peak.*

*The Series 62 ragtop was well equipped, as befits a luxury car. Standard power assists included steering, brakes, windows and seat.* ▶

*The 1959 Cadillac Sedan de Ville was indeed in a "Realm of Its Own."* ▶

Styling could be debated, but few would lobby on behalf of Cadillac's optional (and troublesome) air bag suspension, ordered by mercifully few buyers. Elsewhere under the skin, the '59 Cadillac showed refinements in several mechanical systems: power steering, brakes, steel suspension and HVAC among them. The V-8 was stroked to 390-cid and rated at 325 hp and 440 lbs.-ft. of torque in standard trim. The "Q" engine standard in Eldorado added 20 horsepower.

But with the '59, it always came back to styling. The Rocket Tail put a pointy punctuation mark on the end of a decade remembered for extroverted design. Soon after, though, fins were fine; Cadillac, the first company to embrace them, was the last to displace them. After the 1964 models, tail fins receded back into the fenders from whence they had sprung.

The front of the 1959 Cadillac showed a massive, yet beautiful jewel and bar grille theme.

# Dodge Custom Royal Lancer D500

◄ *The styling introduced in 1957 was improved with graceful touches in the 1959 model year.*

1959 was a tough year for flag makers and music lovers. America's Stars and Bars picked up two more of the former when Alaska and Hawaii joined the union as states number 49 and 50. Rock and roll fans mourned the loss of Buddy Holly, Ritchie Valens and JP "The Big Bopper" Richardson, when the trio died in a plane crash. Don McLean would later memorialize "The Day the Music Died" in his song, "American Pie." 1959 also marked the passing of Architect Frank Lloyd Wright and actor Errol Flynn.

Cars figured prominently in the reigning TV hit, "77 Sunset Strip," and newcomers to the small screen in 1959 included future TV classics "Bonanza" and the "Twilight Zone." New at the drive-in theatre were "Some Like It Hot" and "North By Northwest." "Ben Hur" captured the Oscar for Best Film. Meanwhile, on the world stage, Vice President Richard Nixon and Soviet Premier Nikita Khrushchev sparred over the virtues of capitalism and communism in their Moscow "Kitchen Debate."

Dodge began the last year of the Fifties in 8th place industry-wide, and ended it in 9th place. The company lineup ranged from the $2,516 Coronet Club Sedan to the $3,439 three-seat Sierra Custom Wagon. The top of the passenger car line was the Custom Royal series. A Custom Royal Lancer

◄ *Flaring chrome eyebrows were prominent features of the 1959 Dodge's front end.*

New interior wrinkles for 1959 ▶ included self-dimming rear view mirror and the novel "Swing-Out Swivel Seat." Price of easier ingress and egress? $70.95.

A beautiful Custom Royal ▼ convertible was used in this 1959 Dodge ad.

The Newest of Everything Great! ——— The Greatest of Everything New!

Don't look now, but they're all following you!

Your new 1959 Dodge stands waiting in the drive: Sleek and clean and lovely. You swing into it (via new swivel seats!), close the door and start the engine.

*Now look around you.* There are other '59 cars parked nearby. Friends of yours are getting into them.

*But you and your new Dodge are definitely the leaders, the pace setters, in your group—ahead in every department.*

You are out in front in styling, with the low, crisp Swept-Wing lines that the other 1959 cars seek to copy.

You establish the trend with the taut "look of motion" that other cars are patterned after: The swift sweep of fins, the forward thrust of fenders over dual headlamps, the curving arch of compound windshield.

You blaze the trail of engineering leadership with the incomparable stability of Torsion-Aire ride, the sure mastery of push-button driving, the thrust of your more efficient engine.

*They're all following you!* One sure reward for owning a new '59 Dodge!

'59 DODGE

hardtop like our featured car had a base sticker price of $3,201.

All Dodge models rolled into 1959 on a fresh facelift. Larger, lower and wider than the 1958, the '59 Dodges featured a set of prominent chrome brows arching over the headlights. Meanwhile, two-tier tailfins dominated the rear view, with pointed dorsal fins stretching atop double-barreled taillights.

1958's recession had temporarily taken high performance off the boil, and 1959 would build on that trend with the introduction of new, compact models. But, with increasing market confidence, the horsepower race was rejoined. The "hottest of the hot" for Dodge was the Super D500. Equipped with dual 4-barrel carburetors and a high-lift cam, the 383-cubic inch, wedge head motor pumped out 345 horsepower. Although Dodge rolled 6,278 Lancer hardtops out of their showrooms in '59, it's likely that only a select few (like our featured car) were packing the mighty Super D under hood.

◄ Rocket themes were never more popular than they were in the late 1950s. Case in point: Dodge's 1959 "Jet Trail" taillights.

▲ The hottest engine in Dodge's arsenal was the D500. Versions with 320 and 345 horsepower were offered.

# Ford Galaxie 500 Sunliner *1959*

◄ *Enthusiasts often point to the 1959 as one of most beautiful Fords ever produced.*

SELLING CONVERTIBLES IN 1959 must've been like selling swim suits after a snowstorm. 1958's recession had hit the auto industry (and the country) like a ton of bricks, and one year removed, Americans were still reeling. Convertibles are the most optimistic of automobiles, and tough times are rough times to sell optimism. All of which makes it hard to explain exactly why the '59 Ford Galaxie 500 Sunliner did so well.

Cars that *appeared* in 1959 were *designed* far earlier. Styles were etched in stone (or at least stamped into sheet metal) well before anyone could know

that the bottom was going to fall out of the 1958 economy. As luck would have it, Ford was following their conservative, 1958 styling with '59s that were just a skosh less conservative – not too wild for the subdued, economic climate. The square-shouldered look started with a set of heavily browed, quad headlights.  Parked between and below was a wide grate grille. Oversized round taillights dominated the rear view. While cross-town rival Chevy was making news with wild batwing styling, Ford was largely finless in 1959, playing conservative to Chevy's liberal. Rear fenders were tube-shaped, and capped by a ridge of chrome.

◄ *Ford was happy to promote its gold medal-winning styling in 1959 and it looked especially good on the Sunliner convertible.*

*The Galaxie 500 Sunliner's interior was Ford's most luxurious offering in 1959.*

*Ford ads weren't shy about proclaiming the 1959s as the "World's Most Beautifully Proportioned Cars."*

Ford's "most popular" Galaxie Club Victoria

## The price of popularity is surprisingly low...

Unwrapped just 6 months ago, the Galaxie is today's most desired car. This figures. For the Galaxie is beautifully Thunderbird in looks, power and luxury...yet typically Ford in its big 6-passenger comfort, low price and never-ending economy. Consider: gas and oil savings *alone* can mount to $55 a year. You save because Ford's Diamond Lustre finish never needs waxing. Surprisingly, the Thunderbird-inspired Galaxie sports a price tag only $50 away from a Fairlane 500 Ford. *Only $50!*

ROOMY NEW FORD RANCH WAGON . . . LOWEST PRICED WAGON OF THE MOST POPULAR THREE

Get *extra* savings now during DIVIDEND DAYS at your Ford Dealer's. Special saving dividends plus Ford's built-for-people dividends. Deep springing and cushioning in every seat. Wider door openings are easier to get in and out of. Save up to $25 on double-lasting aluminized mufflers.

59 FORDS

WORLD'S MOST BEAUTIFULLY PROPORTIONED CARS

Designs may have been locked in, but engines required less lead time, and Ford responded to the penny-pinching climate in 1958 by offering motors that were thriftier with a pint of petrol. Lower compression ratios were the rule across the board, so cars could use regular-grade gas. Despite the thrift movement, top-line models like the Sunliner featured here could be had with an available 300-hp, 352-cid engine. The option sheet was further enhanced in mid-model year with the addition of the 360-hp Interceptor engine. It was an early indicator that Ford (and the rest of the industry) planned to shift high performance from the back burner to the front, just as soon as the country's monetary malaise eased.

Ford's two convertibles were headed in different directions in 1959. The visually wondrous (but mechanically ponderous) Skyliner retractable hard tops were selling weakly and would not return. Sales of traditional convertible Sunliners, on the other hand, rose to 45,868, some 10,000 units higher than 1958. It seems that ragtop buyers—and optimists—are hard to keep down.

▲ By 1959, the novelty of retractable hardtops was wearing thin. Sales of them skidded to 12,915, while ragtops rose to 45,868.

◄ The Thunderbird 352 Special V-8 was the "stellar accelerator" of the Ford Galaxie and the 300-hp V-8 was the top engine option early in the model year.

# Imperial Crown

◄ *The 1959 Imperials used a stronger frame that allowed a lower floor and greater leg room inside while maintaining their elegant exterior styling.*

IN 1959, IMPERIAL WAS an automotive David to Cadillac's Goliath. The 17,000 Imperials sold that year compared with 142,000 Cadillacs. Chrysler had spun off Imperial as a separate brand in 1955. Idealistically, the goal was to establish Imperial as a premiere American luxury car line. Realistically, the task was to elbow past Lincoln, and take as big a bite out of the high-end market as possible. Given Cadillac's total segment dominance, the job must have felt to Imperial's brass as if they were trying to shovel their way out of a sand pit.

Considering their upstart status, Imperial had done surprisingly well at the outset. In 1957, its third year as a stand-alone marque, the company had taken the offensive, expanding the brand to three series (plus limos). Imperial, Crown and LeBaron lines were fielded, and a convertible coupe was added (and sold 1,167 copies). Mechanically, Imperial traded the two-speed Powerflite automatic transmission for the improved, three-speed TorqueFlite (which was accessed by push button controls). A power boost was provided to the Hemi engine and Chrysler's fine torsion bar front suspension made the big cars light on their feet. The expansion was

rewarded with expanded sales – some 17,269 units in all. The effort bested long-time luxury maker Lincoln, though Cadillac trounced both Lincoln and Imperial.

As we have seen, the year 1958 was not kind to automakers, and it was downright cruel to those who dealt in high-end models. By and large, people respond to tough times by getting more conservative fiscally, putting off major expenditures, and making do with what they have. Hardly the prescription for a company trying to sell expensive automobiles, and not surprisingly, Imperial sales went slack for 1958, falling to less than half of 1957 levels.

Imperial returned for '59 with a second face-lift on the 1957 design. Always the most serious and least flamboyant of all Virgil Exner's Forward Look cars, the '59 Imperials added a heavy- looking grille, but were otherwise little different visually. Sales rebounded a bit from 1958 levels, but 17,000-plus was still well off the 1957 high-water mark.

Despite fielding a fine product, Imperial was hard pressed to divorce itself from its Chrysler roots. Imperial was new money, in an old money market.

▲ *Even on high-end models like the Imperial Crown, air conditioning was a rarity. Little more than one-third of all 1959 Imperials were equipped with it.*

◀ *The new "wedge head" 413-cid engine was less expensive to produce (and cheaper to keep) than the engine it replaced.*

The Imperial, like other Chrysler products, wore the enhanced eyebrow treatment over its headlights in 1959.

The 1959 Imperial LeBaron Silvercrest four-door hardtop was elegantly posed in this 1959 magazine ad.

Presenting . . . the NEW 1959

IMPERIAL

. . . excellence without equal

The 1959 Imperial LeBaron Silvercrest four-door hardtop . . . fresh from Imperial's all-new plant to host this year's Imperial Ball

Today, America has a new measurement for excellence in motoring.

IMPERIAL FOR 1959 . . . a car whose great dignity is matched by an eagerness of spirit . . . whose luxury and elegance are made richer by a gracious practicality.

A car in which careful interior redesign has provided more space for passengers . . . a car which makes available for the first time front seats that swivel doorward to make entry and exit easy.

IMPERIAL FOR 1959 . . . a car whose farsighted engineering concepts combine spectacular handling ease with a firm sense of absolute control . . . whose newly designed engine develops enormous power with fewer engine revolutions . . . so it need never race or strain or raise its voice.

A car which can be equipped with Auto-Pilot to remind you gently of the speed limit, and to maintain a steady turnpike pace, hour on hour, up hill and down, without so much as a touch of the accelerator.

IMPERIAL FOR 1959 . . . whose spacious Royal Coach Body gives you new dimensions of comfort and enjoyment. A car that comes to you in all its carefully crafted excellence from America's finest automotive plant . . . designed for the utmost in quality control.

IMPERIAL FOR 1959 . . . excellence without equal. A boastful statement? The car is ready for your inspection at Imperial showrooms. See it. Drive it. And then decide.

# Pontiac Bonneville

*◄ The 1959 Pontiac Bonneville was long and lean, yet tastefully styled.*

IN 1959, GM seemed intent on ringing out the old decade with as many wild-styled automobiles as they could muster. Seen in this light, the '59 Pontiac Bonneville – a fine looking car in its own right – positively sparkled.

1959 was the first year of the "Wide-Track Pontiacs." Broader, without doubt: the front wheels stretched 5 inches wider and the rear tread was about 4½ inches wider. Longer and low slung, too. With beautifully balanced lines and less bright work than most of the competition, the '59s had a modern, sporty look, right for the times. In front was the first of what would become a Pontiac trademark:

the split grille. The bold, clean face was likewise balanced by tasteful, V-shaped tailfins in back.

Bonneville was the top series in the Pontiac lineup. It shared the longer 124-inch wheelbase with the Star Chief lines, while the Catalina and all station wagons rolled on the 122-inch chassis. In addition to the sport coupe featured here, the Bonneville lineup for '59 included a convertible, the four-door Vista hardtop sedan and a six-passenger station wagon with an exotic handle – the Custom Safari. The lightweight of the line was the hardtop, tipping the scales at just under two tons (3,985 lbs.) The Wide-Track's broad base and lower center of gravity made these the best handling Pontiacs yet.

*◄ The low-slung lines and road-hugging grip of the Wide-Track Pontiacs launched a sales surge to fourth place in 1959 and third place in 1960 and for much of that decade.*

*The Bonneville showed as much ► flash on the inside as out. Pontiac toned down the exterior brightwork in 1959, but there was still plenty as evidenced on the dashboard. It was like a production version of a show car with a striped jacquard fabric interior and futuristic looking instrument panel.*

A fresh V-8 motor provided the motivation. The debut of the 389-cid V-8 was celebrated with many variations, ranging all the way up to 345 hp , with Tri-Power carburetion. Of course, all that "go" deserved more "whoa," so Pontiac reworked the brake system, adding cooling flanges up front and thicker linings.

Low, wide and handsome, the Bonneville two-door sport coupe stickered for $3,257 and Pontiac sold 27,769 of them. Sales for overall lineup sizzled. Buoyed by their Wide-Track looks and boosted by an economy that had just crawled out of its recessionary hole (releasing pent-up demand), Pontiac vaulted to fourth place industry-wide in car sales. That was 77 percent better than the previous year, and good enough to pass corporate cousins Oldsmobile and Buick for the first time.

A hallmark of the 1960s that began in the 1950s, Pontiac's split grille.

Pontiac upped the competition by doubling the tail fins from two to four.

*furs by Revillon*

THE WALDORF-ASTORIA

Wherever automobiles are seen and appreciated, the Cadillac name has, over the years, become an accepted synonym for "quality". Yet never before has the Cadillac car represented such a *high* standard of excellence as it does today. In its great beauty and majesty . . . in its fineness of performance . . . in the elegance of its Fleetwood interiors . . . and in the skill of its craftsmanship . . . it is far and away the finest fruit of Cadillac's unending quest for quality. We believe that a personal inspection will convince you of this fact—and that an hour at the wheel will add certainty to conviction. Why not accept your Cadillac dealer's invitation to pay him an early visit—for both a ride and a revelation?

CADILLAC MOTOR CAR DIVISION  •  GENERAL MOTORS CORPORATION
EVERY WINDOW OF EVERY CADILLAC IS SAFETY PLATE GLASS

*Cadillac* ...world's best synonym for quality!